Twelve Moons in One Night

For my son Quinn and my family and friends
who have helped within the moons; especially my Mum and Dad

Twelve Moons in One Night

Thoughts Caught in Changing Moods

SEAMUS GUYVER

authorHOUSE®

AuthorHouse™ UK Ltd.
1663 Liberty Drive
Bloomington, IN 47403 USA
www.authorhouse.co.uk
Phone: 0800.197.4150

Published by AuthorHouse   09/25/2014

ISBN: 978-1-4969-9153-9 (sc)
ISBN: 978-1-4969-9145-4 (e)

Contents

CHANGING CALLS ON A CHANGING MIND:

Telephone Call

I

Waiting round for a telephone call,
Pacing up and down watching the phone,
Wandering why I don't just call you,
Stupid pride or not knowing what to say,
Should I write it down and post it today,

II

Picking up the phone so many times,
Half way through your number,
Just to throw it back down again,
Throats gone dry, words have lost their way,

III

Dogs are barking in the world outside,
People playing; talking too loud,
Walking round in circles not knowing what to say,
Would you be glade if I called?
Would you really care at all?

IV

Dial your number hoping you won't be there,
But really hoping your invite me to stay,
I really want to speak to you today,
But I'm too scared to pick up the phone,
Lost the faith and words to say,

V

Spinning like a hula hoop around town,
Every time your street passes by,
Then at home watching the phone,
As all the days roll by making it harder to call,
Wondering if you feel the same as me,
Are you also too scared to call?
Both scared in case we fall.

Token

I

Token for a heartbroken,
Words wished never spoken,
Stop the game, stop the hurting,
In and out you're never that certain,

II

Could we buy this feeling on credit line?
30 days with nothing to pay,
But it only takes a minute to steal you away,
Who knows when we began to play,

III

How many times have you hung up the phone?
Lost the receipt left your token at home,
Heard you're the bad penny of the town,
Hurt the ones you love with a frown,

IV

Everyday just like a burnt piece of toast,
Loving theirs no higher price,
Some people will get it right,
Some will lose never knowing the fight,
Some will never even receive a token,
On times we were left broken.

Yesterday

I

Don't look back at yesterday,
Mistakes already made
Like stones falling into the water,
Memories and actions,
Can never be repaid,
When I stare from the edge of life,
Into shallow waters of our minds,
Yesterdays will be a silent memory,
Ones that can never be caught,
Just think where you stand today

II

As we are caught on so many paths,
Some stopping so short within our hopes,
Leaving us stranded on the bay within,
Some leaving us bitter and taut,
Angered by the choices and chances given,
Making us shake within the darkness,
Caught in stone on yesterday's past,

III

Caught in the shallows; drowning in tears,
Pausing and reflecting on wasted days,
Sitting in the park of spiders webs,
Walking over the hills and cracks within,
Stopping at the edge of the trail,
Looking back upon the dusty path,
Hearing; feeling the voices on the wind,
Seeing the distant light within the sky,
Feeling the tears; shattering your inner walls,

IV

So many mistakes were made yesterday,
So why do I keep them all inside?
Why do I keep recalling them within my mind?
Why do I cut on a paper smile?
Yesterday was a trail within the mind,
Today is the road within my steps,
Why do I turn and burn within my head?
Why can't I forget the mistakes shed in blood?
On a hall or within my own bed!
So many mistakes I thought I'd already paid,
But in the night the scars bleed from the sky,

V

Today is yesterday hanging in yellow lights,
Standing behind the curtain blinds,
Innocence taking within a smile,
Lost in bitter memories and the pain,
Salty waters in a bath of despise,
To the cross nailed upon the bed,
Too haunting thoughts of yesterday,

VI

My yesterdays will haunt all of my days,
Memories of all the games played inside,
To the knock on the door;
Hiding deep within the shore,
Feeling the darkness still creeping within,
Keeping the shutters closed within my life,
Holding a smile as life swings on the edge,
A bitter drop from yesterday,
The loss is there; but will I jump?
As I turn away from all the yesterday's nights,
Step again within the shores of life,

VII

Though the yesterday images scare the brain,
I laugh and cry at the time going by,
I need these lights within my shattered mind,
I need the hanging within my time,
To make me focus on the world today,
Scares are joy and joy is pain,
Ones that make us stronger day by day,
Yesterdays are dark images within my mind,
Caught into today as I slowly move away

Promise

I

Every year a promise to change,
When every birthday feels the same,
Getting drunk in the name of the game,
But a brand new start is what I say,

II

Time to shed my skin,
Time to change the colour of my mind,
Time in which we all have to find,
What lies behind the dreams inside?

III

Of the things we see as black and white,
In the distance sometimes out of sight,
Maybe blurred when we've had a few,
Like an old film when the lines sound the same,
As every scene starts to feel more cold,

IV

Dropping to my knees at the end of another day,
Praying and hoping one day I'll change,
When chained the keys you have inside,
Opening the gates of your mind,

V

Tear of my clothes to start again,
Run naked through the rainy streets,
Burn my clothes and leave them at my feet,
As the rain washes me from head to toe,

VI

A new start but some things will never change,
The pride of things in which I stand,
The knowledge of things that make me a man,
That we were all born of the same hands!

Watching

I

Watching life pass me by,
Sitting on a balcony so high,
Watching the boats move slowly up the Nile,
Like on a sheet of glass,
As the sun dances with the water wild,
Watching all its twists and turns,

II

Till the boats force their way again,
Cutting through the suns diamond haze,
The things of which dreams are made,
As all the liners sit and laze,

III

Then my eyes turn up to the hills,
In the haze of the summer's rays,
The trees bending to their knees,
Or am I just inspired by it all,

IV

From the Nile glistering in a diamond ray,
To the camouflage green of the trees,
In which the houses are hard to see,
Over shadowed by mountains that unites them all,

V

The beauty shines from the ground to the sky,
Is even captured on the people passing by,
A piece of which we all can say,
In which beauty surrounds our lives ever day,
No matter where we stay,

VI

When every towns a coin of two sides,
There's beauty on both sides of the crown,
All it takes is just a single smile,
When shared makes it a length of a mile.

Driving Home

I

Driving home tonight
Not wanting to fight
Knowing only one plight
Difficult way of life,

II

We used to laugh
We used to cry
We used to tell each other lies,
Coming like birds to steal the night,
Now all we seem to do is fight,

III

Driving home trying to remember the times,
The first night I felt your gaze,
To the time we made love till one,
Times we made out on the phone,

IV

Now we don't talk like that any-more,
We just fight like we're in hell,
To the coldest bed were love lives no more,
Wanting to leave but I'm not really sure?

V

So I'll keep driving till I make up my mind,
Maybe were find the love we lost in time,
But the lies throughout the years can't be ignored,
So I guess I must take the chance,
Maybe my last fight falling to my knees lost in the night.

Precious Time

I

Why do I keep wasting my time?
Sitting with people I can't abide,
All I can do is watch skies of grey,
Wondering hoe many hours have gone this way?

II

How many hours have I sat and prayed,
Watching the flickering lights fade and die,
Going in time with my mind,
Wanting to stop at the end of every show,

III

But I don't know where I'll go,
I've walked round in circles so many times,
Sometimes I think I just closed my mind,
Deaf to all the things I hear inside,

IV

Sitting too long caught in a stare,
My minds already running over mountains fair,
Caught in my imagination but who's to blame,
In our life; we must hold onto our precious time!

Clouds

I

I wander why I never saw?
The mist growing in your eyes,
Everyday turning you away,
But in my eyes my loves the same,
In this world how could I be so blind?

II

Even when I looked up into the skies,
The clouds moved so fast in my eyes,
Across the morning sky,
Was I changing so much inside,

III

Why did the dark clouds fill our eyes?
Why did the rain have to fall inside?
But in my soul the wells still dry,
No matter how many tears fall from up high?

IV

From love only a single drop,
Can fill the well so deep inside,
Maybe that's why I'm so blind,
In my eyes the clouds hide the love inside,
Through out the years words are harder to find.

Breaking Point

I

She had me over a barrel,
She broke my poor back,
With all the things she wanted,
Thinking I was just there to pay,

II

You kept me hanging on like a puppet on a string,
Thinking you could treat me this way,
Taking me up then pushing me down,
Thinking I'll always be around,

III

When days were so sweet,
I used to lie at your feet,
When the clouds brought the rain,
To damping all our days,
You sent me away,

IV

You broke my will just for the thrill,
You must have had your heart set on kill,
Bleeding me dry never reaching inside,
Moving on when the money was gone.

Know It All

I

Things you've read in many books,
Words you never really understood,
But talking like you know it all,
Thinking everybody else is the fool,

II

Never questioning the stars at night,
Which light was bright or right?
Only believing what you are told,
Never knowing when your mind was sold,

III

You think you're free or so you believe,
Blind man's bluff were no one can see,
Deaf to the words you don't want to hear,
Only sound you hear is the man on the hill,

IV

You still believe you know it all,
Talk in circles as the melody goes,
Children and money is all you know,
Try to imagine the words Lennon told,

V

If only for one day you would open your mind,
Money is not the only hill to climb,
Talk of love you don't know the meaning anyway,
A little bitch with a pointless stare,

VI

Reading all the loved up books,
Telling of how the perfect love and world would be,
But you don't understand the words or the real world,
No use explaining to a narrowed minded frame,
Look into your eyes and realise there's no one there.

Two Lands

I

Take me to Ireland,
Take me to the silent valley green,
Although I was never born of this land,
I feel there's something there to be found,

II

Maybe it's the green of my Irish eyes,
Or maybe in the redness of my hair,
Maybe there's something within my name,
In the name of the father maybe we're the same,

III

A man caught within two lands,
Both saying you were born of the other side,
Neither excepting me as a child,
Maybe that's why my heart is wild,

IV

But in the mountains I feel I could free,
Maybe there I'll find someone for me,
Someone to share my silent valley green,
To stare within my green and be free,

V

A man not two lands stuck inside of me,
Then to take me for how I am,
In the silent valley will lie,
To hold each other throughout the days!

Thousand Words

I

A face of a thousand words!
Depending on the colour of the day,
The sun of which can make you smile,
Till the dark clouds make you hide away,

II

Every day your face tells its tale,
Every time you smile or frown,
As your face shows the mirror to your soul,
As the words etch the lines in your eyes,
Reflecting the different colours into your mind,

III

Every year the wisdom draws the lines,
Of a million words, in which we disguise,
All of which could be said in just a smile,
In a familiar face where you know the place,

IV

Then in the show your words will glow,
Lighting your face feeling the words start to flow,
Many words are said without a sound,
Told within your smile on your face,
The glow of which compels the heat,

V

So when a face is bitter and torn,
It's just the words are hard to find,
But all we have to do is look inside,
To find a thousand words in the eyes of a smile.

CHANGING STARS IN SEASONS OF MY MIND:

Matter of Time

I

In a short matter of time,
We knew each other's mind,
Always hanging on the line,
Feeling the warmth of passion's fire,

II

Changing our life within a day,
We seem to know each other's lines,
Maybe we met in another lifetime,
Perhaps our lives were destined to pass,

III

Just a spark to light our fire,
Always been burning through the passage of time,
Love can survive all the boundaries,
Waiting for the breath of love
Oxygen to relight our fire,
Love will survive to conquer our desire,
Even the hurt will never leave us blind,

IV

Of all the time it took us find,
The right line within our lifetime,
Now you are here the wait doesn't seem that long,
Suddenly to find a place where we belong in time

V

You know my mind before the words are said,
The letters are on the page to be read,
Running your fingers through my hair,
The lines of love were there from the day we were born,
The fire waiting for us to unite in this passion form

Gliding

I

Gliding on top of the water,
In a sense of grace,
Trying to show our good face,
As we past each other by,
A glancing look to past the time,

II

As our feet kick to keep us afloat,
All we show is the beauty
As underneath the panic sets in,
As we try to find our way home,

III

The roads getting longer every day,
I've waited to long for the train,
Standing alone we've all drowned in so many ways,
In the advertisement the picture we thought we could see,

IV

Is the water pure? Are we really free?
Are we really all afloat?
Can a man really be all he can be?
Which part of each other do we really see?
How long do we dare to stare?
Before the fear makes us turn away,
Just to drift away hoping it will not affect me today.

Losing My Mind

I

Walking upon echoes of steps,
Looking at the images of life,
Feeling that I'm losing my mind,
On conveyor belt of the blind,
Walking, talking about the world,
Never changing in their steps,
Going down further on this escalator ride,
Passing tubes; something inside,

II

Pausing, standing, looking within the glass
Shadows pass within the light,
Hearing past echoes of so many minds,
Voices lost in the air of society
Seeing the explosions that tear my mind,
The love that is kept on a twisted smile,
Seeing seconds of green hills,
Surrounded by the valley of blood,
One we all call this time apart of life,

III

Stand with me if you dare!
Missing the shadows passing by in life,
They will become a blur as we stare,
At the truth; caught on the passing stream,
A dot on the society wall in which we pass,
A hole in which we could all step within,
Small to the eye that has been blinded by life,
Bigger than all the lies we hold inside,
Another world maybe!
With no hate and guns,

IV

I have stopped the escalator of life,
To stop and look through the smallest of holes,
Placing my eye within my mind,
Seeing a distant green field,
Wanting to know what lies behind the scene,
Stuck now in the mirrored flair,
As faces shake at my choice within life,
The coin dropped and never made a sound,
Paused between the chase or the race,
Turning back to the hole within my mind,
If I am losing mind,
I'd rather jump into the pool,

V

To turn from all the greed and violence,
Anther gun down baby in a rocking chair,
A society who choices who has lost their mind,
In the streets of blood dreams,
Feeling the pain within the womb,
Seeing and hearing the pictures within the tomb,
So many chances losing your mind,

VI

Underground in a silent fell consumed,
Fighting for air; in a bubble car
Stumbling through the echoes of time,
Walking down or stepping in sands,
Walking, smelling the lost thoughts,
Standing at the end; as the trains pass by,

VII

The wind whispers in my ears,
Caught within the mirror,

The light on a silent scream,
Drops fall on the bed sheets,
Feeling like I'm losing my mind,
On a street of the diamond light,
Falling from the light to the ground,

VIII

Losing myself on the waters pain,
Stepping in the shade of life,
Stopping on the graves felt with side,
Seeing the crow; tapping on the stone,
A pictured flight on the stream,
Fishing for the ones that make us believe,

IX

Now I have been caught in the nets,
Stuck in the Walters of my mind,
Sinking down; within the time,
The pain within a lost in shadows
On the light and staring in the night,
On water dreams that met the scream,

X

Now I'm losing my on sugar clouted dreams,
In the streams of the past,
Losing my mind within the stream,
Lost in caught of the thought of the mind,
Travelling back in the thoughts of head,
Time to die within a losing mind,

XI

Losing my mind on shattered dreams,
You smile on the cracks of life,
Falling tree on splinters green,

Wondering, still standing at the bar,
Too slow; watching the mirror screams

XII

Stumbling into silhouettes of echoes,
Feeling the shadows long gone,
Ones stood in the corner of the mind,
Tiny finger prints on an empty tube,
Passing faces within the clouds,
Wondering what does it all mean?
Families running over the green,
Blue light as the liquid washes upon the street,
Feel like I'm losing my mind in all this confusion,
Watching the cracks appear on the grey walls,
Catching keeping us within this hopeless dream,

XIII

Rain falls on the blue light mind,
Hearing the bells within the flashing lights,
Blood on the floor; was it there before?
Fish at the door; with a jacket for me to wear,
Spinning clowns on a merry go round,
Finding me already nailed to the ceiling
Spinning in the darkness within my head,
Losing the light and track of time,
Moving forward in my thoughts,
Stuck in the stars and moon within the night,
Laughing as the fluid drains from my brain,
Caught upside in a backward world,
Spinning anti clock wise upon the hour,
Motion is movement; on the ceiling going no-where
Losing my mind on the board of spinning dice,
Wondering if I shot a six or two,
Wondering if life is really fair!
Or have I just lost the hatter within my mind?

Searching

Sitting in my room; staring at the wall,
Searching in the distant specks,
Ones caught within the blind stare,
Stuck in the middle of the chair,
Listening to all the echoes within my mind,
Seeing washing streams upon the walls,
Feeling the drops echo within my mind,
Slowly moving within the streams,
Caught in time,
Lost in the shadows of my mind,
Searching for the shadow,
That has danced within my mind,
The spilt within the sky,
Chasing moons,
So close within my mind,
Time on a ship; stood still
Sadness of the mind
As we search in the bodiless of life,
Cuts and thoughts on searching dream,
Feeling the blue eye's turn in sting,
Playing the music within your mind,
Dancing still on searching light scream
Playing the music in the night,
Caught within the moods of the sky,
Searching in the stars,
Lost searching within the night,

II

Searching within the sky
Searching within the night,
On a mind caught within the blue,
Feeling the moon within the shadows,
Dancing in the streets,

Caught within my changing moods,
Searching within the moonlight sky
Skipping in the shadows of life,
Searching in the valleys of time,
In hands and wounds of shattered memories,

III

To search in this life,
For the thoughts on the line,
Images caught within the sand,
Searching within our different moods,
Always drowning within the seas,
Chorus
It's the searching
That keeps searching,
In the sparks,
Reflecting the stars,
Caught within the
The sparks of your eyes,

IV

Feeling the motion of the searching,
Makes me feel high in the darkness,
Makes me feel low in the stream of light,
Feeling the beat of the air,
The wings that link my heart and soul,
Feathers lost on journey long ago,

V

Searching caught within a tune,
Different sounds within the night,
Flashing lights and images,
Searching for that one single beam,
A face; a place or a hill within,
A drop of light to quell my torched soul

As I flick through the pages of my mind,
Searching to find the place I lost in time,
To find the small thoughts of hopes,
Lost in a child standing alone,
One caught on the edge of the void,

Chorus

It's the searching within me
That keeps me from falling down,
In the sparks caught in the sky,
Reflecting the stars,
Caught within my head,
The sparks of my eyes,
Makes me search again within the void,

VI

Searching in the scratches within vinyl thoughts
Images that dance in Midsummer night's dreams,
Caught within a swirling head,
Sitting still; but spinning on a thread,
To the lost tunes and faces within the sky,
Searching for the button to stop the ride

Strain in our eyes

I

Clouds walking upon the empty streets,
We move slowly through so many eyes,
Caught within the stream of life in time,
Shattered upon the speckles of the stones,
Walking fast seeing the reflections in the mirrors,
Of the strain of life; hope and dreams of the past,
Left shattered on the walls and memories
Thoughts of what might have been!
In shadows caught deep within the darkness,
The line keeps pulling at the strain inside,
Leaving us stuck in a place,
A time; where the footsteps stopped

II

Meeting different faces on the pavement of dreams,
Stepping into the shallows of the wells within,
Pausing; focusing on the distant looks,
No words or smiles on a sea of waves,
Knowing in a glance we have changed,
Saw a new road on the path of life,
Turning in the breeze of time,
Seeing the childhood look within our eyes,
Lost within the strain of life we feel today,
Wanting to capture those lost; distant times,

III

When we walked through the night,
Talking about what life which held us inside,
Seeing your eyes reflected like the sky,
Now seeing the shadows that cover the night,
Running; but standing still in time,

Wanting the strain to disappear from our eyes,
To feel the hopes and dreams we made yesterday,

IV

We must keep walking within the mist of time,
Pausing looking into the well within us all,
Faces pass showing the hands of life,
Drowning within our minds,
Blinking to the images that keep us alive;
Wondering why we must face this strain in life,
Turning as the splinter reflects within our minds,

V

The line of life is cut so deep within us all,
From the people we have taken to our hearts,
To the streets we have stood for a million years,
Our soul is old and the strain is vain,
We keep chasing; wanting new dreams and hopes,
Looking at life feeling the strain within our eyes,
A frozen caught on the edge of a bulb,

VI

Watching the changing flashes on the screen,
We watch the people come and go
We stand staring into the vacuum of time,
Wanting to step within the void within,
Feeling the strain that pulls like a cluster of time,
As life takes a hold of your body and mind,
Keeping me skipping on the edge of the moonlight sky,
As I feel my body fall and start to dissolve,
In the atmosphere within your mind,
Feeling you need to set your soul free,
The thought bulging within your eyes,
A moment of time, a sea within the screen,

Knowing you must be free from all the madness within,
As the strain in your eyes spots the blood inside,

VII

I am left sitting in my bed,
Looking through so many eyes,
The childhood dreams and thoughts,
Chasing the skeletons walking through the night,
Hiding in the clothes in the wardrobe shirts,
The silent noises within the sky,
Never reaching to find the shorting star
The one left so distant within my eyes,
Flashing in the mind; sky and thoughts of the mind,
Passing like the looks within so many eyes,

VIII

So I now look within the strained eyes,
Caught in the shower; left naked in the rain,
Silent drops shatter on the path of time,
The red mixed within flashing with the lights of green,
As I feel my life dissolves, like sugar paper in the views,
Keeping me walking on the shores of time,
Taking me so far within the strain of our eyes,
Chasing the waves; keeping us looking,
To horizon and feeling we could be much more,

IX

Now we step on the sandy beaches,
Feeling the strain with our eyes,
A trail that has to follow our thoughts,
Keeps us steeping upon the sand,
Lost in the footsteps within our different times,
Knowing we must break from the lines that hold us,
The single lines outside our window,

The travel of the past,
The future seen through so many strained eyes,

X

Now I step within the back of my eyes,
Capturing the thoughts that skipped through time,
The beat of the person I wanted to be,
Reflecting of the images that show within the wells,
Posters and chants that scream within the mind,
Standing on a bridge with no ending or beginning

XI

Seeing so many eyes within the stream,
Looking the pains of the eyes,
Standing on the bridge,
Lifting as the roads and minds within,
Stepping across the barrier,
Being pulled within the strain within my eyes,
Feeling the blood within the streets,
A silent drop; smashing in the waters below,
Skipping on the beach I have climbed so high,
Feeling the never strain in my eyes,

XII

Now I have stood; riding the time within life,
Staring over the edge of time; in the blurred scream,
Stepping through so many different doors,
To face the faces that holds the strain inside,
Feeling the pain that will never subside,
Like chasing the boat within your mind,
Though I know it's just a matter of time,
To swim with the ghosts that 'I HOLD INSIDE!'
To never feel the strain within my open,
Closed to what I see around me,

XIII

Now I stand in the rain,
Felling the shadow of the man,
Caught in the past of flashing lights,
Missing your smile and held in blue light,
Seeing the drops in the puddle,
One caught within the soul of life,
Turning my eyes to wish for a brighter sun,
Feeling the pain; droplets that full from the sky
We hide; we shine in the moonlight sky,
We bleed; we wipe upon the scarlet scene
We stare in eyes that show so many thoughts,
We strain to see the eyes that make us complete

Roads:

I

Past is the time that clicks within your mind
Turning a corner or seeing the line
Echoes of the past kept deep within inside,
Climbing trees, smelling the summer breeze
To a broken glass held within a flask
Within days of speed; captured within dreams
On splinters of glass holding so many faces,
Echoes of the past; the silent screams within your mind,
Take you down a road you've never known
Left staring with winter streams

II

Staring at the tombs of the past,
The line of the caught river dreams
Running away; but never travelling through your roads,
An empty place caught within morning glow,
Passing the willows that reflect the thoughts inside,
Stillness of the day as you keep the thoughts deep down inside,
Moving from one house to the next,
Slowly the people start to climb and fall

III

The paper falls; standing alone in a hall
Willows whisper in the summer breeze
Snow will fall on the wheels of time
The path is clean; but the hill is high
Calls from the stream will make us laugh and cry

IV

From the church to the bottom of the road,
A man will climb upon the hills inside,

When you're full the hopes are stuck within,
When you crewel all you can feel is the ground in which we tread,
When you are high we reach above the sky

V

The passage of time will reflect the roads we have climbed
Through the empty streets in a paper dream,
To the solitary roads we walked within our minds
Time wondering about the first kiss,
Time with friends on the empty streets,
Roads that hold the secret dreams within,

VI

Willow may drop within your mind,
Though streets are blind within your thoughts,
String at an empty wall,
Talking to people who have never walked upon the road,
Road that changes through every lane
Turning a corner within your mind
To pass the footsteps held so deep and pure,
Feel the walls and slogans we both laughed and cried

VII

Roads may have changed; but we are standing still,
On a paper round at the break of dawn
On a time of a train caught without the jeans
To a time sitting alone watching slogans on the wall,
Passing through the changing roads of time,
The sleepiest dreams; roads within my hands

VIII

Now I walk up empty path,
In my 40's staring at a reflection in my mind,
Feeling the steps; hearing the cries,

Of the past and dreams held inside;
Standing reflecting on the roads,
So many times; thoughts held within,
To stare at the sea or the person held deep within me,
But the roads may change,
These thoughts and feelings still remain within,
Of all the passion and visions held within my soul,
So I keep on walking upon the roads
Feeling the steps will change within my mind;
Hoping that time will change the streets to a better place,
One felt within a silent dream,
Street of dreams; on mind that is clean

Journey:

I

On a journey were the roads will never end,
The ones of which always drive me round the bend,
Returning all the letters in which I sent,
Even to the house in which I grew as a boy,

II

The lights of which never seem to be far,
Some of the lights broken on a single path,
From my bedroom window from which I stare,
Even in the light the darkness I was scared,

III

Through the ever changing seasons,
Touched by the sun and the rain
Through the times in which I shone,
Sometimes spring come early to my eyes,

IV

To find the start half way through my life,
Understanding the words within my head,
My dreams visions of things never said,
Telling of things of what could be,

V

On a merry go round bringing me back round,
To see and learn from the things never seen,
To the house I lost myself as a boy,
Trying to find the place in which I fell.

Love Age:

I

Could you really be mine?
Nothing in age only state of mind,
Generation lines and time never show in eyes,
Loves strong some things were meant to wait,

II

A gap some will find hard to bridge,
To cross may only take a step,
Both consenting holding within a breath,
How many years do you wait for a soft kiss?

III

Was it fortunes wish to still be alone,
Maybe a game on a hand already played,
Love kept blind until the right time,
Chance meeting on things never seen before,

IV

Never heard church bell's chime.
Happiness is not made on what over people say,
But on an identical tune heard in the heart,
Happiness passed within a touch of a single smile,

V

Time has no concept when love is born,
Take you by surprise in a single look,
Hitting you like a speeding bullet from a gun,
To bring you to life the way only love knows,
Age is the only difference in which you hold.

Fallen:

I

Fallen angel touched by heavens sun,
Tear drifting upon the wind,
Feather fallen from a wing,
Kiss upon the gentleness of skin,

II

Hold the string of the first tear,
In emptiness of a lonely soul,
Heart strings played on a broken guitar,
Life was a song played on missing notes,

III

Broken heart stuck on repeat,
Day of words I don't love you any-more,
Love was a fool who rushed in,
But to love for a single day,
Worth the emptiness of all the days that remain,
To hear angels sing then chime no more,
Is better than being deaf praying for loves sweet moan,

IV

Funeral March one step in your heart,
Things never seen when unborn,
Angels and devils lost in brown eyes,
Pleasure and pain no blood will remain,
Scarlet days when angels fall in vain

What's Wrong With Me?

I

What the hell is wrong with me?
Did I arrive too late, second class?
Spent too long in rosy clouded dreams,
But life's too hard for these things,

II

Strangest thing in the world,
How to make a girl like you,
More than just a friend
Make you feel the same way I do,

III

How do I make graffiti fall like holy rain!
How on earth could I make you stay!
Kiss your picture till the break of day,
Knowing you don't care and would never stay,

IV

So why the hell can't I move on?
Laughing like a clown like you do,
Stepping on people for your own gains,
Tossing them aside when you've taken all you can,

V

Vampire when loves like blood to drain,
Black hearted when a ghost you drag around,
So the hate of love you try to kill,
Well you carved out my heart laughing in the night,

VI

Watch me fall with friends I thought I had,
Now I see the turning meaning of their masks,
Love I still feel though thinking what the hell's wrong with me,
Memories must be hanged left for dead in the night.

Loser:

I

Born into a continues losing streak,
Never knowing when the race begun,
Like a three-legged horse at 100 to one,
A long shot bet which no one will take,

II

I've seen people's eyes
Turn away too many times,
Making me turn away inside mine,
I want to change my face today,

III

In and out of love like a man who never wins,
Is it just fate, or the hand you were dealt,
When every day you just hate yourself,
No longer willing to stare at your own face,

IV

So when you have lost the race within,
When your home never feels that clean,
Are you at the end did you know when it begun,
Even as a child you never had much fun,

V

When you feel your coats a different size,
Cut your hair but you still feel a mess,
Every day you feel you have to break away!
From the chains you hold within your mind,

VI

Everyday who are we really trying to please,
Your gentle hand will always keep me at ease,
Telling me I'm a winner and not a looser today,
Even on the days I turn away wanting to hold you close.

Happy or sad?

I

Am I happy or am I sad?
Can you feel my different moods?
As you read the lines within my thoughts
Do I change or remain the same?
Can you see the moods reflected within my eyes?
Do you believe I am holding a distant smile?

II

Are there many tears within my soul?
Can you step and feel the waterfall held within?
All mixed within the joy captured in my mind,
Can you travel through this book?
Hold your own peace of mind!
Touching the inner thoughts you hold inside,
A journey through time and space,
A path within the soul we hide deep inside,
A journey to a place you may not wish to find,
Steps within the thoughts and emotions within your soul,

III

Silent words on a journey within the mind,
Which some may find it hard to find,
Some may leave it in the corner of the room,
Some may journey and feel the demons they hold within,
An open mind I hope you hold inside your soul,
Take my hand and follow the journey throughout this book,
To open up and hold the different lights that shine within,

IV

Do my moods change or stay the same?
Am I content within the world in which we play?
Do you sometimes feel the same way too?
Staring in the mirror that changes in time,
If so the journey I hope we will share,
Bringing light to the feelings we hide within our soul.

TIME NEVER LIES IN THE ESSENCE OF STARS IN THE SKY:

Games

I

I work in this place,
Hardly my mind in idol talk
Baling finding my mind,
Lost in the shadows of time,
On the waste that hits the ground,
Stuck on the greens of the past,
Searching in the void of space and time,

II

The shattering bombs on the tombs,
People clutching the babies in our eyes,
Games played on wasted years,
Walking in silence upon the hills,
Left me standing with blood on my hands,
Working and slaving upon the mill,

III

Now I'm caught in the game,
In this place within shattered dreams,
Wasted on the view of pictures within my mind,
Of all the fantasies I wanted to climb,
Lost in the game; that dies in the memories

IV

Playing games on a spinning board,
I could the superhero in the sky,
A hell raiser smashing T.V. screens,
Floating upside in a pool,
A big football hero,
Pouring champagne through glinted glass,

Playing the game on the mist of time,
Screaming from the tower block,

V

Feeling the hammer within my hand,
Wanting to smash the games in my mind,
Left sitting in the red of so many sheets,
Smashing it down; chasing the clouds,
Moving slowly around the edge of town,
In a painted smile of a clown,
Keeping close the shadows in mind,
Seeing my face within the weeds,
Caught on the stream in time,
A game played left laughing,
As the man drowns within the weeds,

VI

A boat moves in the caverns of time,
A chance to walk against the water spill,
In Kubla Khan in bitterness within my mind,
Never seeing the flecks of life,
Feeling the games with faces I see,

VII

Sitting across the table; or standing outside,
Wanting to stop the game,
Cut the line within my smiles and broken eyes,
People wanting or searching for something,
Believing they know what's best for me,
They will never see the rope that hangs from the sky,
Now the game just keeps them smiling,
When I am hanging in the window of the darkest light,

VIII

The games left me standing in this place,
People looking at the floor,
At the teacher who preachers
Shouting trying to escape from the lines,
That holds the madness and escapes,
Never wanting to hold the candle of life,
Watching the shattered games within echoes,

IX

Now we stuck in the halls,
A girl stepping on man's lies,
Games in the playground have gone too far,
When close to the shutters in our minds,
Left me standing on a basket court,
Left in the shadows of the winter's tale,
Games in a tale on feelings inside,
Shouts in the corner of the room,
Now I'm stuck within the games that we play,
We all one step from the curtain,
That hangs in time,

X

Stuck in games,
Never hearing the shore,
Left in this place,
Of false smiles and words,
Keeping me shattering on the rocks,
Sinking deep within the waves,
Playing on the dice that never throws a six,

XI

Now I am caught on the board,
In the games of other people's hands,

Sitting shattered in walls,
A splinter screams within the hall,
Paused on the hatter on a board,
In streets of yellow dreams,
On a dice; within a game,
Now I have shot the bullet brain,
Shattering on the eye within my dreams,
The game lost in this society of hopes,
To the lectures; stuck within a hall,
Games played within the crowd of people,
The ones who never regret the time within the mind

XII

Now the doors are open wide,
Showing the hanging dreams,
On games on the Broken board,
The mouse has run to the cheese,
Left us standing on the game of life,
Caught in the traps within the game,
Holding the waves within our heads,

XIII

We talk to the people within our heads,
Stepping; crossing on the waters,
On the game within our shame,
We walk through the trees,
Wood cutters of visions in the sky,
Dark blurred eyes make me standing,
On the edge on highlights in my eyes,
The game I have played,
Are the stones in life!
Shattered within the South island class,

XIV

Walking too or beyond the gates,
In the light on the beam,
Games played standing on the edge,
Dominions fall in inversion,
To the blink of an eye played within the game,
Walking in and back through the door,
Seeing the edge of the production line,
The stream of thoughts never gone,
Feeling the game in the mist of time,

XV

Left sitting on Old Kent Road,
Stuck within the hold of a dice,
Maybe a double six will move your feet,
Snake eyes taking you down upon the streets,
Paused broken on a shattered board
The diamonds never show within the sky,
Smiling as the dice hangs on the side,
Walking in shallows of the mind,
Stepping everyday within the game

Times

I

Life seem harder to face,
All we do is argue about money,
And about this tiny place,
These are our days,
As we pray one day we'll escape,
But when everybody feels the same way too,
Many minds have turned to vacant skies,
Some turn to drugs to help them on through,
While some turn to crime to take all they can,

II

But your love will always keep me true,
In your eyes we're never be blue,
We're leave the world outside and hang on tight,
When all we've got is this love, we're hold on every night,

III

Though at times our love will feel so low,
As we lose our way not knowing which way to go,
All I need is the slightest touch of your hand,
Your warm breath to keep me still,

IV

But at times I just can't face the bills,
Going insane thinking I could kill,
Then on my neck the hand of which I feel,
Knowing as long as were together,
We can keep away the chill.

In or Out

I

Flickering light dark but bright,
Changing times near but far,
Waterfalls echo of babies cries,
Kisses shock near misses,

II

On a plane light year from Mars,
Speed of sound words never found,
Friends of the past who come last,
Standing still or running fast,

III

Tidal wave on a summer's day,
Skipping in and out of the rain,
Live in sandcastles you've made,
On waste-ground in which we played,

IV

Times will change from yellow to green,
Some things are never as mad as they seem,
Holding onto a piece of string,
Pulling or climbing all kinds of different walls.

Money Hole

I

Debt that needs to be shared,
Children choking on instead of being fed,
Deeper hole which only brings death,
Generations being born into the red,

II

Onto a land that's already been bled,
War destroying their homes in which they fled,
Now all that's left is a land of tiny holes,
Families left to shiver in the cold,

III

Digging in the land with their hands,
A man hoping to feed his family one day,
To be able to hold his head up high,
Surely the feeling we must all try,
To release the chains from around the world,
End the pain what we call the money game,

IV

Big fat cats on interest rates,
Squeezing the money from the people,
In a mixing bowl bleed them dry,
Every single penny who cares how many die,

V

In a money hole all they want is pride,
Stop bleeding them dry,
Give them a chance to rebuild their lives,
Pound of flesh you can't take much more,
Give them a life not a money debt.

Green God

God from a machine,
In a shade of the paper green,
A promise to pay the bearer all,
Keep us climbing upon the wishing tree,

Wondering who's got the biggest TV,
Take out a loan if that's what you need,
Saviour on the end of the phone,
Inadequate feeling if you don't have the biggest car,

To some love is how much your worth,
A different meaning to say your green,
Pray for it then squirrel it away,
Brag about how much you can spend,

Pray to God or money in the end,
As long as you got more than the people next door,
People starving but you've seen it all before,
All you do is pray on the balance on the cash machine,

Fill your house with gadgets galore,
Be the first to buy the newest machine,
Spend your money on crap hold your head high,
A shallow person until the day you die,
God will ask you how you helped mankind!

Young at Heart

I

It was only yesterday
When I was only ten,
Playing out all our dreams,
In the play ground and muddy greens,
Time when I was young wild and free,
The world was my own little playground,
So many things I wanted to be,
But inside I still feel real,

II

I never believed all their lies,
But sometimes I fall to my knees,
I played the game and got scared,
Will I ever get the blood of my hands?

III

I wish I could turn back the clock,
But which one of us would I warn,
Sometimes I feel battered and torn,
In a war where the scares kept me warm,
I wouldn't change a day on paths we strayed,

IV

Today will be our yesterdays in so many ways,
Dreams will be reality if we learn to play,
Time has no concept in hearts that are free,
So young at heart is how I'll always be.

Decisions

I

I could have stayed at home tonight,
Alone to watch the big fight,
Sit in with a take away and a tin,
Play some music dance around the bin,

II

Maybe take a chance in town,
Let my hair down and fool around,
Meet some friends who will take me in,
Never knowing we might even sing,

III

Slur my words when I'm on my third,
Now I've even spotted a bird,
A smoke and a drink and I'll give her a wink,
Talk for hours on a pleasant smile,

IV

Tender kiss when it's time to leave,
Take your number a promise to call,
A right decision to go out after all,
Fate bounces us all like a ball.

Eyes Closed

I

People lining the streets,
Some haven't enough to eat,
Money saying it's too much to be ill,
As you feel the world start to close,

II

A game of poker where some will fold,
But not the ones who dealt the hand,
As some of us try to make a stand,
While others will hide all they can,

III

In this world of milk and honey,
Being old or stuck on the dole,
Being born on the wrong side is no longer funny,
When everyone's fighting for a piece of the pot,
Turning back the clock to the Dickens day,

IV

So many footsteps in the snow,
Where do they all go?
Generations that has died in the cold,
Building for a future in which was sold,

V

And yet we still close our eyes,
As they tempt us with more and more lies,
Caught up in utterance of words,
As we fight to hang onto all we can,
All hanging on an old shoe string,
Within the system of the greed we made.

Everyday

I must leave my love so lonely,
To fight for foreign lands,
For the things I will never understand,
But I know I will always feel your hand,

II

Miles may keep us far apart,
But your always be here in my heart,
When we stare up at the stars,
The miles will never seem that far,

III

We can hold each other's hand,
As we both look and see our hearts,
Are shinning on the brightest star,
Wishing you weren't so far away,

IV

If I have to die here today,
I hope you know I love you more every day,
If I fall in the lands so far from you,
I'll feel your hand hoping your hear my words and understand,
As I feel my body die but my love will never grow cold,

V

I know our love through our baby will grow,
Hoping he'll find the love I miss every day,
Praying we will all find a better way,
Never to die under another man's hands,
When through peace we can all share the same lands.

Reflections

I've always stood on the outside,
Reflections of faces I wanted be,
Of all the people in which I see,
Sometimes caught like a song on the breeze,

II

Always two steps behind the crowd,
Clumsy and loud in a silent town,
Seeing reflections in people's eyes,
Not of me but of what I wanted to be,

III

Always dreaming I could be someone else,
Turn around with a different face,
A man of cool, Instead of a clumsy fool,
A popular man with girls on hand,

IV

Then I won't have to talk so loud,
Just to attract the crowd,
A shadow of a man stumbling around,
Never fitting within this town,

V

As we pass the windows, I see,
Reflections of things I wanted to be,
Instead of reaching for the goals inside of me,
As the passing time reflects in my eyes,
Always praying I could have another time.

Tracks

I

People say I should search around,
Go out and find another girl,
Get my head out of the clouds,
Get back onto the track,
To a place where I can fool around,
But I don't want the hurt any more,
And I don't care what people say,
When their lives are patterned out,
2.4; with kids around their feet,

II

The mortgages getting them in deep,
As they get stuck within their own feet,
Stuck within the factory heat,
As they plan out all their weeks,

III

But my goals are way too high,
And I still feel I can fly,
Not realising my wings have been clipped,
As I'm floating through the air,

IV

Wanting the joy and pain,
Women to take me by the hand,
To hold me throughout the night,
To kick me out when we've had a fight,
But most of all to fill the lonely void,
Above all else just to keep my feet on the ground,
Too keep me sane,
On the track were my train will glide.

World Outside

I

I could roll over and die,
Close my eyes to the world outside,
Sit alone in my room,
Watch the world from my view,
Or I could find a better place to be,

II

One day the scares will heal,
Then my broken heart, could feel,
All the days lost in my mind,
All things I never done, things never said,

III

As I stare at the world outside,
Thinking I should have been born in a different time,
Watching the children play on a tiny green,
Where we played all our hopes and dreams,

IV

Has the world changed since I was young?
Or has it always been the same,
I remember playing football in the rain,
Turning round and the world had changed,

V

In my eyes things could never be the same,
But I must keep striving for a brighter day,
Open my eyes and face the world outside,
Another day, hope and pray I'll find a better way,
No matter what they say we can all have our day.

Blue Eyed Boy

I

An ocean skipping the skies of smiles,
Reflected upon so may open faces,
Flashes in the sea; that hold my mind,
The waves crash on the rocks below,
Washing me to the shore once more,
Stepping through a life on the horizon,
Seeing the changing moods in blue eyes,
Captured on the whit; tanned sprinkles of life,
Left standing; sitting in a green open space,

II

Droplets falling upon an open face,
The sea and sand reflect the changing seasons,
Of a blue eyed left staring at the sky
Feeling lost; long tear drops never falling,
Of the past; roads once held in the lines of hands,
Showing and knowing the tear drops,
That falls like silent screams within the ocean,
Speckles on the waves that smash on the shore,
Feeling the sorrow; wings of so many dreams,
Blinded within a soul,
On an empty earth of life and destruction,
Knowing in the streets I will never find,
The blue eyed boy who chased the clouds,

III

Now the summer falls within the rain shine,
Seeing so many eyes within the dark skies,
Searching within the moon and stars above
Drops falling upon an angels face,
Seeing the streets and hearing the screams,
Half closed to the madness, in which we see,

Knowing we only hear only half words,
Told to us as we step upon the rain dropped streets,

IV

Now I sit in the corner of my mind,
In streets of time and passages within my hopes
From the lights on the puddles within the talk,
Of people who never step within the shadows of time,
Jumping within the blue eyes within our being,
Reflecting on the violence and silence within my life,
Standing on the neck,
Lost in the hopes and sting within the mind,

V

A blued eyed; green sea of man,
Lost in the swells of tears,
Falling down as I stand on water cliffs,
Wondering if the scooter has flown over the edge
Falling within so many blue eyes,
Seeing the pebbles smashed,
A boat let on the river stream,
A lonely finger facing a blue eyed boy!

VI

The boat has stooped on the journey,
The one caught within the dark sky,
The tear falls; but never hits the ground,
Never to quench or hit the ground below,
A blue eyed boy with so many dreams,
Skipping through the shadows of time,
Caught within the twelve moons of images,
Making my eyes water in the shadows

THROUGH THE TUNNEL

Through the Tunnel

Part 1

I

The drop of light falls at the start,
Sitting under the sink drinking bleach,
Smashed mirrors on torn knees,
Running fast through the woods of time,
In the dark tunnel of the mind,
Giving the last rights when I was four,
Still moving through this tunnel of life,
Hearing echoes of the crashing car,
Making me turn to face the empty walls,
The one held inside in my shattered mind,

II

The tunnel is high and full of demons in shadows,
With laughter of boy smashing his head,
In front of mums; the pain made me smile,
Carried through the halls by a blond in disguise,
Flashing glass takes my thoughts away,
Women dressed in white through the lights,
Trying to patch up the head split from within,
Staring at the green; caught in the tunnel,
Seeing the holes within the timeless faces,

III

Another section of the tunnel shows the pools,
Running across the sand chasing a shadow,
Seeing a thousand eyes in the water sky,
Being pulled out of the or pool,
The air was gone as time stood still,
Pumping hands made the air spin again,
As a mother looked within the sky,

IV

Walking in the tunnel stopping at these visions,
Cracked on the edges of the wall,
A shadow creeping in the room at night,
Mixing on the sheets within a youth,
Stuck in the house of God,
On bended knees asking for forgiveness,
Drowning in the salty bath,

V

Making me turn from the edge of the light,
Caught in this tunnel; but moving in steps,
The smoked full room body on the floor,
The pictures falling from the walls,
As the lights flash on the edge of tunnel,
Feeling the air and mask placed within the air,
The beat stopped in 87 as lights flashed in the sky,
Sections of shots as the doctors thought for life,
Second time to have priest by my side,
Closing eyes trapped in the tunnel of time,

VI

The skull makes up the tunnel,
Cracked and scared in the pain of life,
Left sitting the bubble of the witches and ghost,
Seeing the light beaming in the distance,
God calling me to the edge of the tunnel,
Thought I wish to stay lost in memories,
Of all the trickles that fall,
From my head to my feet,
Laughing in this tunnel of shadows,
Touching wings that have tried to bring the light,
I see their distant wings fly,
Through the tunnel I sit and feel the droplets,
Falling from my body on this world of heat,

VII

Turning to step in droplets of blood,
Washing my body on the trickles of the drops,
Dancing in the pain of the shinning blade,
Caught on the floor in pool of blood,
My head stuck on the urine white light,
The two parts of mind split in the tunnel,
Staring at faces as the liquid falls from my mind,
Boys in blue asking me questions on the ward,
Laughing as my brain mixes in the tunnel of time,

VIII

Standing behind the curtains of a seventh man,
Feeling the nails holding me to the wall,
Sitting on a scooter seeing over the edge,
Cutting names within my veins,
A sharp pain caught in the shoulder blade,
Laughing in the tunnel of this red stream,
Caught in rooms on the edge of many different beds,
Seeing faces; but the faces are blurred,
Like the scares trapped in the tunnels of my life,

IX

I have walked through this tunnel,
Left empty fragments of my brain,
On the shore of bitterness,
As some may think they can relight my life,
On the screen and people in the wasteland,
Searching I hope for their hopes and dreams,
Ones that never me shake the tunnels of time,
Caught through the pleasure of life and pain,

X

I have traveled through this tunnel,
Seeing the light; turning back,
Never wanting to the feel of sheets,
To feel a beat or heal the feathers of time,
When I think back again on times in the grave,
I want to lie with the fish within the sky,
Can we ever make it through the tunnel of life?
When we are trapped on the scares of the stones!

XI

Now I press on the water dripped streams,
Feeling the drops fall on my body,
Turning from white to red,
Scars open in the shadow of the room,
Seeing the tunnel move upside down,
Walking to the light on the horizon,
Not what others wanted in my life?
Trying to find a person to take my hand,
But the drops are all I want to feel
Staring at hole that has my name within the cloud,
Falling fast on the tunnel in my mind,
Washing through empty streets,

XII

Walking back within this tunnel,
Seeing faces passing me by,
Walking to the light,
Smiling as they past the haunted dreams,
Closed within my smile and hiding eyes,
I show on the doors of my life,
No emotion in the sky,

XIII

Never step in this tunnel of time,
It's a place for just one man,
Trying to capture the inner demons,
It will break you spirit on the sky,
You never want to be me,
Hanging on the edge of the tunnel,
So don't make your friends walk in the distance,
When you know I will hang them in the tunnel of darkness,

XIV

Now you may never see the light behind the green,
I am lost the lights of dance floors,
Standing still in the middle,
Caught in the tunnel,
Splinters of the brain caught on the walls,
Walking through so many lights,
Drowning in the seas of time,
Never try to capture all these thoughts inside,
Never walk within the tunnel of my mind,
You will die on the drops the splinter the soul
You will walk to the light of the stream,

XV

Never touch my hand or see my hidden smile,
As I flash back to the hidden thoughts within,
Caught in this tunnel we walk through,
Sitting on the mild tomb,
I will never change on the green,
Day's standing in salt waters,
Blessed upon a bed or the flashing lights,
Broken on a floor in the stream,
Walking through the tunnel with no light on my head,
How many us will find the edge of the tunnel?

XVI

Now I'm sick of the light on the hall,
Stuck in the bath water filling my body,
Sick of the windows and shadows everyday,
A silent scratch brings the waters fall,
To stop the walk in the tunnel within my mind,
Stop people talking of the happiness within my thoughts,
I want to swim; sink within the weeds,
To drown through the tunnel of hiss dreams,
I am dead on these different walls,
So walk through the valley,
Never turn back and see a smile,
When the blood may you sting
Cause I'm dead in this tunnel of lost minds

XVII

The tunnel is caught within several thoughts,
The tunnel is long with the drops within my mind,
Smashing silently on the road,
Falling through the mirrors of changing lights,
Caught in the tunnel,
As the steam of red; shocks green eyes
Carve set within the stone,
Taking me back to the grave,
I wish I could die on the cross,
As the rope snatches within my neck,
The light shows the darkness within,
I would rather on the beams,
To face you on a lonely bed of hopes and desire,
I would rather hang in the tunnel,
Full of shadows within my mind,

XVIII

I'm dead hanging on the washing line,
Running fat to see the light,

Turning to see the middle class smiles,
My blood has been lost,
Shattered head on the venal; white steam,
I would rather be here staggering,
Trying to the walls upon the walls,
Rather be me standing in a pool of blood,
Seeing the light within the tunnel,
Now I am dead in the tunnel,
Seeing the light,
On the shinning metal scrape,

XIX

You can wish the steps in night,
But you never see the darkness in shadows,
Keep me walking in the mist of light;
Seeing faces caught within the stream,
I wish every night I take that knife,
The blade gleams on the green streams,
I have been dead since 87,

XX

You may see the smiles on the corner,
I hope you travel in thoughts of my mind,
To see the sky and broken visions within a tunnel,
Wanting to fly and see the sky,
Falling in the waters that show so many green,
Dying through so many so many rocks
Now I have walked through the tunnel
Stopped on the light that never shines,
Now caught within the dead of dreams,
Games placed on a darkness scream,

XXI

The shadows of flight in the night,
Keeps me walking in the sight,
Love to feel the cuts within sudden blight light,
The drops in yellow street lights,
I wish I could die in the moonlight sky,
I am taking the fluid and the shinning bade blade,
Reflected within the tunnel,
Stuck on knees as my brain starts to bleed,
Wanting to die in this tunnel of flashing dreams

Through the Tunnel

Part 2

I

Days sitting on a train,
Light reflection upon an open glass,
Crawling through tunnels on Saturday grass,
Shooting in the wind on Ashe open glass,
Running the stream with clouds within,
Hearing the Bees; but never feeling the sting,
Coming home on minds that were cold,
The one who said we will both join in time!

II

A flame sparked within the flashing wind,
Ghost from the past who wrote a 'Broken note!'
Stopping the pain or caught in a frame,
The tunnel is deep within the heart and mind,
The blood flows like so many bottles of wine,
Dead before I hit the door on a needle time,
A long lost memory within a hall,
A so called friend taking into the wall,

III

First there were days I played in the rain,
In caverns you kissed and held my name,
We danced in the changing moons,
We thought until it was dawn,
On bended knees and within a rose,
I asked you to stop all the madness within
You took the ring; but never brought the stream,
My own fought as we clashed in the night,
The tunnel was my only port of life,

IV

Knowing I destroyed the grain within my hand,
Closed the doors and sat on heavy steps,
Liquid nights staring into the dark,
Shinning blade was my only friend,
Wasted years with blood on my crown,
Wandering round like a clown without a face,
Standing still in the tunnel within my mind,
Caught catching time on a fisherman's line,

V

The 20's are a blur to me,
Wanting the head shakes and bees within,
Still feeling the nights all alone,
On a scooter carving a name,
To the rides from the riverside amusements,
Dancing naked in the valley walls,
Working two jobs just to make you feel the same,
Broken again on a tunnel that will never turn

Through the Tunnel:

Part 3

I

Sitting deep within the tunnel of my mind,
A light reflected deep in 96
A Christmas dance out of the glance,
Roberson and Jerome played the classic song,
You stood on the dance floor by your own,
I took your hand and held the melody inside,
We danced until two,
Your blue eyes made me sigh,

II

A promise to meet you next day,
Fear although captured me in the morning dew,
You waited there; but I never showed,
Too many years in the tunnel to climb outside,
Standing on a hill; so deep within the tunnel mile,
It may have been months to I saw you smile again,
Glasses free; and blond waves within
Bluest eyes and a smile that reflected the sky,
You spoke to me and my tunnel shown no more,
Deepest kiss and smiles you could never miss

III

We danced for some time,
Until the tunnel once entered my mind,
You're shine turned away to another man,
As my soul turned to walk in the tunnel of my shame,
Feeling warmth; is not the like coldness of your time,
Bleeding arms are better than a closer friend,
Within the tunnel I drift and move along,
Crashing and hearing the sounds
Of all the bells that have gone before

Through the Tunnel:

Part 4:

I

Inner Demons had come to me,
Silent wind within the skylight
Promises of hopes and future dreams,
Nothing promised without a curse,
On red wine and salmon meals,
A friend that meant so much
Disappeared without a trace,

II

Left me cold in the tunnel; once again,
Sitting staring at the blood on the walls,
Surrounded by regrets and the wolves hale
Never wanting to go back home,
Happy to stand out in the bars that are all the same,

III

Then I met you my Australian friend,
Caught in nurses you come to play the game,
Velvet trousers made you find the fun,
Kissing until the moonlight had dropped from the sky
Number on a cigarette tube!
How could I know which to dial in time?

IV

the call on through; you spoke like a charm,
I thought the tunnel was now closed behind,
We met at the bus stop; not so romantic
Rugby was your favorite sport
But I liked cricket no big deal!

John and the boys they loved from the first meet,
All should I should make your wife;
Even my mum was the first to agree,

V

But the tunnel called out to me,
A distant echo within the shadows
A silent cry somehow lost in the night,
Half the world separating our fondest dreams,
You set sail for your homeward sun,
I sat down in this tunnel within my mind,
Trying to find the light to show the way

NEVER DOES THE MOON CHANGE THE STARS IN MEN'S EYES:

Freedom

The ship stoop still upon the ocean,
The chains clicked, shimmered and fell,
Hopes sat in the darkness of the hole,
A vision caught within black and white,
As freedom rocked on the empty shore,
So far out to sea,
For the naked eye and brain to know,
Freedom lost in many waves and speckles in time
As the ship stands still on the white of the waves,
Beneath the sea are the green footholds of time,

II

Sinking in the footsteps in the sand,
Burning within so many foreign lands,
Seeing the boat move down the stream,
With so many skins on the helm,
So many bodies and faces staring upon the sky,
To wish to float in freedom of the tide,
We stripped the land,
Made many eyes turn in the night,
Things fall apart on heart of darkness,
When we lose the notion of freedom in the mind,
A culture destroyed within the bush,
Gain of the green that seemed so good,

III

We have flowed within stiles tides,
Brought the chains and slaves,
Cut down and killed the lions eyes,
Stuck on the wall within our pride,
Slow moving feet on black hands in chains,
Who never talk of the Christians bells!

The ones that took the freedom from the well,
As they dance within the chapel hall,
Turning from the ghosts of freedom within the fields,

IV

We sing like God full folk,
Under a cross of a man who died in pain,
Who wished and blessed the sinner on his right,
But we are on the left stealing, lying all the time,
On a Friday or Sunday calling to the Lord,
Taking the freedom of man caught in the sand,
Holding the child fighting for rain,
A single drop may keep away the flies,
But we stand and take all we can,
Leaving a boy soldier caught in the rain,

V

We enslaved a nation full of greed,
Spilling the same blood within a Roman sword,
The drops speckle on the fallen ground,
For we hang so high; when freedom is lost in our minds,
On colour of skin do we hide the lies?
Pestles that fall within the moonlight sky,
Enslaving the people in the North and the South,
Freedom will never see the burning flags,
We will never stop the moon and the ships at night,
If we don't stop the hate reflected in the steps of time,

VI

Hate will tear us all apart,
Freedom will never come in three nights,
A ghost of a man brought after life,
A line in the sand which we can never cross,
When we turn our guns upon our friends,
In a religion divide on flags within the sky,

Knowing we are all the same,
The thorns may twist within the mind,
But the cross and distant remains the same,

VII

I may stand here dead,
My blood has shattered within the sky,
I still see freedom on the rocks' and silent boats,
Still believe in the words of so many preys
Caught on the night within the cross,
As my blood drips within the thousand,
Caught freedom of the blood that never stops,
Falling like a tidal wave upon the earth,
As freedom of pain; pain of freedom is lost,
A sudden call in the night,

VIII

They say that humans have rights,
Though we are nailed on the wooden beams,
I love the pain; though I can't stand the scene,
Of brothers walking dead within the sea,
My flesh turns to green,
My eyes fall from the sky,
When freedom is took from mother's cries,
I just sit here watching the boat stand still,
Hearing the blood on the waves,
The rocks smash my head within the night,
Freedom is just a cross carried on the time,
Sinking deep within the moonlight sky,
I wish I could be free not trapped within the seas,
Of all the hurt we cause with bombs and stones,
So I must die within the green seas of time,
I laugh and cry as freedom shatters in my mind

Bloodstone

I

Build a dome on essence of man,
Eleventh don't forget to remember again,
Innocence in which died so young,
Fought out on a house of cards,

II

Upside down money joker disguises in many eyes,
Torched earth drenched on river of blood,
Poisoned seas not just a human grave,
Rallies that send men to their deaths,
Something in which happens on both sides,

III

Revolution in which to help mankind,
Filled the pockets of ones who told lies,
Poor sold on a production line,
Working underground for somebody else's gain,
Tossed aside when they have taken all they can,

IV

Wars not the only thing that kills community lines,
Children sweat boxes still here today,
When moneys worth more than a human life,
Just keep us eating from the same bowl of greed,
Establishment knows you're always pay with your blood,
Money in which they gain on your bloodstone!

War Cry

I

A cry for independence,
In the name of a rose,
Muddy fields blood does flow,
For the reason only a few do know,

II

Centuries of revolution history cries,
Bloody crusades in a holy name,
Replace the man with someone the same,
Save a tear for those who died in vain,
Future sold for somebody else's gain,

III

War to end all wars
When you kill half a million in a day,
Heroes would be better of alive,
Too many fields do their bodies lie,
Lies told on either side,

IV

End the wars before the final bell,
New millennium penny for a wishing well,
Wake up with no need to kill,
To be equal in each others eyes,
Life's has to be worth a little more,
From the womb to end with a bullet from a gun,

V

First we must win the war,
Inside our own hearts and minds,
Defeat the hate, greed and despise,
Let love in our hearts shine,
Let peace be our war cry.

Empty minds!

I

You talk about war!
A social fight in the sky,
Talking with your empty minds,
As the stars rush in the night,
Hitting the place a baby eyes stare,
Wishing upon a star,
Left without an eye that can see,
Filling so many minds with hate and despise,

II

Flashes of light on the television screen,
Burning the night as empty minds unwind,
Smoke in the air as people stand and stare,
Empty of the thoughts,
As the light breaks another home,
Never seeing or hearing childish cries,
A youth caught behind the shattered stars,
Bouncing everyday within his mind,

III

I wish I could see a brighter day!
Where the stars never shatter on the earth,
When love and peace will shine the way,
We either find a way
Or dig a hole for us today,
Join the hands to stop empty minds,
In shadows we hear the children's cries,
Knowing the shadows and echoes are not far away,

IV

We have seen the blood red sky,
Flames on the distant hell of life,
Touched by the brinks that fold within us all,
The police and army race upon the wall,
The shots in the night on the battens drawn,
To a mother shouting within the sky,
For the blood that has left empty minds,

V

How can we watch the falling skies?
Within empty minds of streets of disguise!
Knowing the shame is caught within river beds,
Traces of life never caught in a bed,
A face of child caught behind a block,
The sting of the words within empty minds,
Shock on the hall were blood lies down,
to the tomb of nature and men's lies,

VI

Pain of the cross I don't hear no more,
Stains on the sheets within three days,
Within the block within our minds,
A resurrection upon the sheets,
Time to turn our empty minds,
When blood; like sheep fall within the sky,

VII

Now my blood has fallen in the sea,
I no longer believe your eyes,
Or see within the ten mile climb,
When your hate destroys the vision in my mind,
Calling back visions in an empty mind,
You battered me for the lives that are free,

Caused me pain on a balance in life,
Your empty minds caused violence in the sky,
But there was lorry that made it through,

VIII

Know I don't want you're calls in the night,
My blood has dropped within the fire,
Seeing the violence dance in the night,
Caught on empty minds,
Shattered on a toilet floor,
Seeing the images of man with bomb,
Under the walls on broken stream,
Of men holding the stones thrown within,

IX

Leave me in this empty mind,
No longer believing in the world of hate,
Trying to find the peace,
Knowing I will be shattered,
By the empty mind,
Stuck in the clouds of an assault clause,
Be the first within my empty mind,

X

My brother has seen in the waters,
Both are dead on the line we climb,
Stopping to feel the water inside,
Of the life's caught in the shade,
On my empty mind that echoes in the sky,
I am dead within the politics' greed,
Wish to die every night on blue screens,

XI

My empty madness shows the war inside,
Listening to empty words of N10,
Leaving me in the shadows of so many eyes,
The brown thoughts of football dreams,
Mixing in the red within the sky,
I dance so free within the spectrum,
My empty mind see the scares,
As I lie upon my ghost dead bed

Why!

I

Why do people have to flee their homes?
Why do we fight with hate in their eyes?
Why do we kill a man waiting for a bus outside?
Why do some of us think we can stand aside?
Why do we watch women and children die?

II

Why do we look to science to kill a man?
Why don't we help each other all we can?
Why do we poison the air in which we breathe?
Why do we hide chemicals within the sea?

III

Why do we hunt everything we see?
Why do we cut down the forest for our greed?
Why do we put a price on a baby's head?
Why do we let others starve or freeze in their beds?

IV

Why do we follow fools like sheep with no heads?
Why do a few dictate the way we are born bred and fed?
Why do we pump drugs into animals to make them grow?
Why do we mess with Mother Nature, though people still starve?
Why don't we see were all one colour?
Why don't we except that everybody's believes are within ourselves?

V

Why don't we stop hate, killing the child inside us all?
Why don't we join hands and make this planet our home?
Why don't we banish greed by sharing the wealth of the land?
Why don't we stop the children asking why, tears in their eyes?
Why don't we show them joy, not how to destroy?

One World

Children on parade with a gun,
ABC's killing much more fun,
Fighting for freedom
Fighting for deliverance,
We should all pray for forgiveness,

II

Third world or one world,
Depending if you're rich or poor,
Freedom is something can you afford,
Do you know which class?
You were born into before,

III

Children playing in genocide,
Way of life killings not a crime,
Lost youth playing with a gun,
It's no longer a game when people really die,

IV

Mob killing people in the street,
Sold to the people on tongue full of lies,
See how the car bomb blows your mind,
Teach the kids how to despise,
Instead of love and the joy of life!

Justice

Justice in the name who?
Hands on the walls in the night,
So many youth standing staring at the walls,
Caught in thoughts of justice for us all,
The stop and search gone beyond the wall,
The blue lights scream in the lights,
Makes us stare and wonder on justice at all,
When the light shows the dead in the clouds,

II

The law changes to suit the few,
The batten changes in the line,
Upon the youth that held so many scars,
Caught on the streets that holds no dreams,
How can we reach within the sky?
When the justice of the line,
Makes them stand holding to the sky,
Seeing the dark shadows cover up the moon,

III

Free of will may set our minds free,
We both must clean up our streets,
Stop the drugs and silent voices within,
Justice can be achieved when we hold down;
All the guns and crimes within our minds,
Stop the shooting within a cab or the night,
To never see the tears within children's eyes,
A social person who walk within the stream,
A teacher who stares upon the walls,
As justice claims the life's we have never seen

IV

Free to walk in the streets,
Like a pine stepped in the new dream,
But we are fools to know that justice,
Will not kept us staring at the walls,
As the wooden stop people will always,
Keep our hands hanging the sky?

V

When the law is in favour of the few,
The sword is blind to the people,
Who make the sight of society?
A gold dream on the street of the law,
Chopping the heads of ones that are small,
Leaving the ones who are caught,
Laundering millions on a bank scam,
But we hold the fill within their greed,
Letting them use on second sentences;
But justice keeps the black man down for thirty years,
When he holds a pound within his pocket

VI

Now the justice says we come from broken homes;
The bad streets and under paths
Images and slogans within the mind
Against society and the holds within,
Passion of a youth within the mind,
Against the justice that makes us scream,

VII

Innocent being framed by the law,
Sudden shots in the blue sky,
A body left under a sheet,
A family destroyed on thirteen lines,

Who will clear the red shines eyes,
Clean up the dark mist echoes of the streets,
To hold and build the darkness in the slums,
To tell the youth who hold dark thoughts,
That justice in blue will call in time
Tell them that never stand again,
A wall just because the colour of their skin,

VIII

The law is blinded in favour of the few,
Tax wind sharks in the night,
Taking a million within a push of a button,
Lost hopes and dreams within a pen,
Money gone within a single night,
Left standing in the rain of justice,
When one handshakes another,

IX

Left judging the ones from broken homes,
The mould on the walls and chimneys falling down,
With so many scratches on their knees,
A forgotten place and race,
Who never step within the justice of man?
Left in the cold of societies dreams,
Falling sick within the ever increasing mould,

X

Innocent rain falls on the growing streets,
Of hands and minds shattered in the rain,
The youth of innocence being sold on the street,
A girl who has closed her eyes upon the world,
Seeing education a false salt in the sky,
Time to sell the only thing she has,
To the ones who poison the rain?

XI

Who is going to clean up the slums?
So many generation projects,
Rising and disappearing in the street streams,
Leaving echoes and minds turned from the light,
Watching each chance and project dissolve in the rain,
Hitting the empty one room shelter of the law,
Left them in shadows of the halls,

XII

Only we can change our ways,
When justice only seizes the bright of gold,
We must stop killing ourselves within the hall,
In the flickering bulb of the streets,
Time to stop all the ends and post code wars,
We are all brothers born under the same sky,
Justice must come from us!
If we are to unit within peace of a brighter day,
Then the law will never be blind,
Judging a man by the colour of his skin,
Or within the road in which he is born,
Stopping the blood shed on the streets,
Never to hear the screams of justice echoed in the night,
Of the families that bleed in the stream,
Justice for all or none at all

Slogans Within Walls

I

Coloured slogans; writing on the walls,
Saying this is their home,
Don't even think you can stay,
People living in fear of the few,
But there's much more you can do!

II

Lines of contours on a map,
Estate soon a Police state,
Take down the walls and slogans you hold,
No matter what colour we are all the same,

III

Religion should never be a divide,
Tolerance is the only way to survive,
Division of thoughts and beliefs,
Should never stop the way we feel and live,
Listen to both sides and agree on peace,

IV

We only talk with a different tongue,
When our minds are closed to the meaning of unity,
Don't be frightened by the drugs and the thugs,
Unity is a slogan we should display on the walls,
Fresh foundation on life we shall build,
Under a flag of different cultured hands,
With the Police who will protect and serve,
A government not afraid to mean the change,
Join our hands and show that we are all the same,
New world, a promised world, not a broken world!

Job Today!

I

I want a job today!
I don't want to stay this way!
This empty box may be my home right now!
Vacant space in this time and place,

II

On this path in raindrops I have chased,
On the wind to chill an angels face,
Tear drops on a wall gone without a trace,
Maybe the wind has changed within our minds,

III

In the bells maybe there was a chime,
Something said within the writings on the wall,
To the grey streets in which we tread,
But to some it's their life and home,

IV

We're not far within our steps,
Caught within a game the pawns are the same!
So why don't we head the call?
Never listening till we take the fall!

Forbidden Dreams

I

We hang in the green of so many dreams,
In a world that holds so many thoughts of hate,
Blood dripping in the sands of time,
Eyes with so many flies,
Scattering from our so called dreams,
From the blotch in the sand,
Of tears that makes us bleed,

II

Forbidden world, forbidden dreams,
Seeing the tears from brown eyes,
Never touching the bitter earth,
As we watch the bullets fly in the sky,
Leaving in a world so mean,
Seeing the flags and banners fly from so high,
Full of pride and hate,
Keeping us trapped in the views of forbidden dreams,

III

Bang! Bang! Go the guns,
Fear of love; fear of peace,
Of the people who walked upon an army,
The ones who marched for a better life,
Blinkered on the television screens,
Keeps us long from the fear of peace,
As the walls shatter down within our minds,
A Sunday chase on the blood within the streets,
Which will always keep on the killing grace?
Chocking in the flame of a gun,
Killing the eyes that hold within the sky,
Why can we never shake the forbidden dreams?

IV

We are own our knees,
We must stand together and fight,
Not with guns; hate and despise,
But with love born within the sun,
Find the lines that unite our hands,
When under God we are all the same,
The child beneath a same burning sun,
Never to born on red eyes within dark skies,

V

We must and fight upon the tears,
That has shattered the rivers inside,
Not with guns and hate despise,
But with the walls that held us inside,
Walking slowly on the tombs,
The diamond sky says we all the same,
Born in the sands or on the plains,

VI

Though we watch the world apart,
A man hanging like us within the trees,
Watching the world tear itself apart,
Through the winds and fields of genocide,
Killing dreams; hopes in minds,
Only seeing the silent drop in children's eyes,

VII

Forbidden breams on a world that spins,
Never stopping on the rain,
That never falls or shatters within eyes,
As nature angers within our crimes,
Waves burn and shatter in the night,
Telling it's time together and climb,
Beyond the blood within the clouds,

VIII

Build a world within the valley green,
Find a place; within all the same smiles,
A place we can call our own,
Rebuild the human race on different plane,
Far from the forbidden dreams of yesterday,
Full of greed and hate cultures lost in time,
Say these thoughts are not hollows in the sand
We can change, build a new foundation,
Forgetting the forbidden dreams

Home Pit

I

Enclosed in walls of a prison cell,
Keeping in the drug pit hell,
Who's the ones you're locking within,
Police were never meant to kill,

II

Big brother built on fear,
Closing in the watchtower up high,
Community gone by the by,
Left out on the refuse
A forgotten pile,

III

Retreating further into our homes,
Saying one day we'll escape from the pit,
But the wolf will follow you all around,
Don't wait for him to come knocking on your door,

IV

Stuck in a coliseum show,
Christians and lions are just the same,
Just using different sides of their brain,
But only they can stop the game!

V

Break down the walls inside and out,
Show the children drugs are not the way,
Unity in community will set them free,
Even the ones who don't believe,
Who don't live on the estate?

VI

Think there above all that's ill,
But the wolf in the pit,
Has no illusions on who to kill,
Like a leech it will seek and suck out any life.

Social Disease!

I

Social disease on veins that bleed,
From a tower block no future seen,
Empty mills on gravestones of steel,
Escaping reality on a needle thrill,

II

On a journey destined to return,
Track to drive you round the bend,
Skipping in and out of reality,
Till you don't know which world your living in,

III

Skies will never always be blue,
When a city has turned to grey,
Disease spreading must be cut away,
It's not trendy or a social thing,

IV

Locus we must destroy from underground,
Some of which we already know,
Gangsters, police, politicians who watch the scene,
All have their hands in the pot of the social disease,
Selling a needle and gun to every home,
Not just the so called broken ones,

V

Young and old we all have to turn,
Life may be hard but deaths not the way,
At first the fast track may seem like fun,
Until your no longer the one driving the car,
Stopping when you're hit the bottom of the hole,
When only death can come from social disease!

Pondering friend

I

A memorial of a pondering friend
A record playing something short,
Bag of rags hiding a childish smile,
Footsteps tapping on the turnstile of the wild,

II

Cleaning the street at your feet,
Bluest skies in seagulls eyes,
Speak in the eye of the smallest fly,
In a night when dogs begin to howl,
How many wolfs are loose; starting a brawl,

III

Skin and bones just behind the door,
Peeping Tom without an eye,
Ring it twice till the red light shines,
Every year the fair will appear,
As the dead grow nearer to the end of the day,

IV

Window cleaners in early morning dew,
Picture seen threw a hazy draw,
Cattle pushed ever closer to the door,
Leaving me here with my thoughtful friend,
Was the youth worth the sacrifice on time of old?
How would you view this scene at all?

V

My pondering friend,
If you could stand and tell the tale,

Capture the spirit of man;
Would you talk about the sacrifice?
Tell a tale of life's sweet delight,
Caught in the hand of one who has given so much
Lost in the days as life never showed you the show,
Maybe the people will turn on the box; and see their mistakes.

VI

You sit and ponder on the earth;
You take your time; considering life's sweet decline,
Of all the teachers who hear your words,
Talking about the life in which you changed,
Never knowing or feeling your tears,
Of the sacrifice you have endured,

VII

Now you sit here on the land,
So many faces stare at your broken heart,
So many words are spoken in your voice,
How many know the terrors you endured?
Shot within a week of peace!
A man of fire, peasant's desire!
You took the oath and cried to sleep!
You witnessed the death of your fellow man!

VIII

To talk in class to read your verse,
Believing they know the sacrifice of you all,
We hear of the wealth; people who knew how to express themselves
But the working classes are blind to the sound
Of all the people who took the oaf and died without a word,
But how many of us will head the call?
Middle class teachers' talk as if they had felt your pain!
Unfolding your words; within limited brains!
Like a fly caught within a spiders wed!

Only knowing the empty views told to them,
From another middle class teacher,
Who has never see the grain or horizons within the mind,
Crying in vain; trying to imagine your pain,
They take the time to read your verses,
Take the time to stand and watch you fall,
They cry, hold a poppy in your name,
But they will never feel your hurt, love and desire.

IX

In a class room we talk in verse, structure and key themes
Holding your thoughts and dreams;
Missing the beat of the heart; lost in the snow,
You try to reach the people, who have fought so hard,
Died on the cross of time;

X

Peasants revolt to the cry for the rights of man,
Staring at the raindrops in the ocean
The madness you feel and see at the end
People standing in a line of resource and guilt
Of words you thought and carried so deep,
As the strangers past like skeletons in the night
So this may be the scene
This may a change of life,

XI

You may never understand the words or slogans written on the walls,
Time is a change and life will always change
Teachers talk in bold field the lives of the fools
To change a conflict into a blessing
Your gods stood watching the passing time;
To stand with the people who felt the same;
But your thoughts were higher than their dreams
You thought you could be a man in time;

A reflection of the water stills
A time to hold the; hear the breeze of winter trees
A time captured in your bed or in your head

XII

Now you stand, sitting looking upon the earth;
We all stand frozen in time
Pondering on a thought;
We all consider the times of life;
We all consider the dreams and hopes we had
To travel on this journey upon life;
Staring at the roads we face
Like a child who never feels disgrace

XIII

To touch your face in the morning light
To feel the pain, you suffered and endured
To know the silent screams you held within
Is to touch the life that keeps us within our own soul
Will we never end the pain inside?
Will we capture the love, sweet desire you held within
Will we just hide the light from our eyes?
Standing still, what love remains?
A friend to heel the calls of us all
As we pass in single fall!

Horse Dance

An image flashed out of the sun,
Beating down; lost within a stare
Gone never hitting the ground,
A ghost repeating within the mind,
From the past left long behind
A dance of the horses free

II

A time spinning within the mind,
When fire and water held the balance of life
When the mountains shook to the different dances
Of the mane that run through so many hills,
The only call was the one to be free
Not the call of man to destroy all we can find

Chorus

The trail of the hoofs is left in the sand,
Taken back by the spirits that holds them so deep,
Leaving the only sound of the horse dance,
Skipping in the dance of the tribes that held their spirit,
Holding them in the songs and mysteries of their lives,
Destroyed by the ones that never knew the price;
As they travelled from the roars of the sea,
Never knowing the beauty they took away

III

The horse dance is caught in the valleys of dreams,
A valley only few can travel within
The catcher of dreams and all our souls,
Silent faces within outspoken lands,
Seeing the land destroyed.

To the rows of the many wheels,
Hearing the distant sounds of the horse dance,

IV

The silent voice within all the madness around,
Sometimes makes us stop and focus on the wild,
Some people caught scratching upon the earth,
Not for food or greed,
But to hear the steps of the dances before,
Feeling the echoes stuck so far within the earth,
Shattered by the cries and the bullets that fly,
Taking the dance that once held this world,
Keeping the balance between man and his own species,

Chorus

The trail of the hoofs is left in the sand,
Taken back by the spirits that holds them so deep,
Leaving the only sound of the horse dance,
Skipping in the dance of the tribes that held their spirit,
Holding them in the songs and mysteries of their lives,
Destroyed by the ones that never knew the price;
As they travelled from the roars of the sea,
Never knowing the beauty they took away

V

Caught within a culture of greed and survival
Expanding within the land of the dances
Taking the heads and teeth to heal man
Giving the youth a gun and the right,
To shoot a creature who has always stood tall,
To protect its family like we all will do,
Not for survival; but for sport

VI

What will we do when we no longer here!
The horse dance caught within the wind
When the scallop no longer brings the sun
When the land is left no more without beauty and sound,
When the trees no longer bend to the wind;
When we are not let within the valley of the hoofs,
To see the joy of the dancing horses

Smell the Flowers While You Can!

I

Who has the most?
A man with all the land!
A man with a single grain in his hand!
A man who takes time to listen to his children?
A man who will be there no matter what the cost!!
Although most of us chase the God like pound,
Never taking the time to stop, and see what is really around.

II

Who is to blame for making us think this way?
In this race we have no time for rest,
Some may say more is less!
Who knows the time, or where we may eventually stand,
Equality I thought the politicians said!
For the ones who come from the same line.

Chorus

Reflection is the mirror of your soul,
To pause and to count your days as they go,
To consider the beauty and time in which we hold,
To be free and remember the day,
To smell the flowers while you can
To enjoy and care for the ones you have today,
Is part of the universal thought of life!
A gift is given even if we don't see our true flight!

III

Who focus on the common sense of today?
Words of the past that echo through each generation,
Simple thoughts of women and men,

But to hold the thought is to hold your time,
Freedom of man is the knowledge of a society base!
But who holds the keys to knowledge of your fate?
Who will see within the grains within your hand?
Who will spell and explain the motions of the wind?
Who will take you to the place you want to believe?

IV

How do a Tyler and Bull speak of justice for all?
In nine days how will you accomplish justice for all!
Maybe minorities being the mass majority,
Who work and slave for the privilege every day,
Smell the flowers of the lies that we've been told,
Who makes a stand and says we can be the best in which we can?
Ali, Parks, Luther King, Paine, Marley, Gandhi and Eric Thomas,
Staring at the empty promises in which they stand,
For money is greed and money is what we need!
Who take the power of the green?
Who can take the shame of the disgrace of being poor?
We sell our future and youth on greed and pain!
Who knows the answers to make us sane?

V

Reflection is the mirror of your soul,
To pause and to count your days as they go,
To consider the beauty and time in which we hold,
To be free and remember the day,
To smell the flowers while you can
To enjoy and care for the ones you have today,
Is part of the universal thought of life!
A gift is given even if we don't see our true flight!

Imperfect!

Do I want to walk on the paths of the empty dreams!
To scatter the hopes we have within our minds,
To explain myself on the AP of dreams,
To search on the impact of time!

II

Searching for the impact that relieves our minds,
We walk so closer to the walls,
Those are paper thin within our souls,
Easier to see the disguise within our minds,
To stop and stare at the people above;
Feeling the change within our own back doors
Time on a step
With the imperfection that shines inside,

Chorus

The impactions within our minds,
Stood; staring at the ones who talk too slow!
The ones that never held the grain within their heads,
Of all the people that state they have shown,
Now the imperfection are built within or heads,
Standing still; on the light of a mill;
No more thoughts caught in your head
As the imperfection colours the stream of life,
Now you are caught within the words in a class,
A sudden of dreams; caught within the stream
A clouded life on the paint within the mind,
In a rush that has no street lights
On the imperfections of the ones who held you;
The ones you thought could hold you above the clouds;
Only to see you hand in the distant trees,

III

The spot on the hand of man,
We all see the speckles caught in the land;
The one of sand; so trapped inside the soul,
Images on the faces dancing on the walls
With a gun or spear to take the life we hold within;
Imperfections are seen in the deep colour of the moon,
Blood is the sky; light is the mind

IV

How much we step impersonations within our minds?
To see the hunger and despise!
Never breaking the paper walls within eyes
To save the ones who stare upon the well,
That has seen a single drop from their eyes;
Now we are left standing in their shell,
Of all the drops; we once within our hands;
Now lost on the earth we call 'History time'

Chorus

The impactions within our minds,
Stood; staring at the ones who talk too slow!
The ones that never held the grain within their heads,
Of all the people that state they have shown,
Now the imperfection are built within or heads,
Standing still; on the light of a mill;
No more thoughts caught in your head
As the imperfection colours the stream of life,
Now you are caught within the words in a class,
A sudden of dreams; caught within the stream
A clouded life on the paint within the mind,
In a rush that has no street lights
On the imperfections of the ones who held you;
The ones you thought could hold you above the clouds;
Only to see you hand in the distant trees,

V

Now we are caught within the streams,
Of the imprecation that hold so many screams;
On a march of peace within a Sunday so cold;
To a man shot within his single room;
A payer gone the lips of society;
To call the peace within every man
To loose so much within a society divide an American dream,

VI

So many shots that have blinded our dreams,
So many imperfections caught on the stream,
The reflected light of the walk in the street,
The stars and flags; stars in the skies;
We die; we hold the skies above;
For only we can see the imperfections we hold deep within;
Choices in life that keep us from the stream!
That holds the deep imperfections within

LOST IN THE MILKY WAY IN SHADOWS OF THE MOON:

Passing

I

On the passing street
Steps falling from your feet
To a house held within your mind
Passing ghost in the yellow street lights
Staring at the visions of you;
Caught in a land and time with no sunlight
The dust trickles on the wind
The place to which it all begun
To the hole you feel the sky enfolds upon your mind

II

Dust may settle upon the winter change
Staring at the clock in the darkest night
Red glows flicker the minutes of your life
Time to change or change in time
Sleeping through the hours that remained
Passing the people long gone within the passages of time
Some have made you laugh and cry
Some of which you may have died
Although the passing is life and loves sweet delight

Chorus

Life is passing on a train with no lines
A journey to find the person you hold within
To a place and time where the light shone within you
In dreams we see the vision within ourselves
On a dusty road you pass yourself in no disguise
Naked within the moons sun beam
A child of the earth; but without a light
To stand within the beam without a word to say
To wish to follow the dreams washed away long ago

III

Days and nights are passing within the palm
As people and time enraptures your mind
In the snow or the sun it's a place you find home
To the scars that a brother stung deep
To a man who with a bat in his hand!
Talk so deeply and no lies within his eyes
The passing of time is wink in your eye
Staring across the street as life passes you goodbye
On the buses streams of life such delight

IV

We passed in this town or someone's life delight
Clouded room you took me by the hand
But the loves was yours; but never mine
Passing like lovers in the beam of light
To a room where you called me a fool
Brothers are all around as now!
Too the won we must count as clown
Passing is life and life is time

V

The music has stopped, but we travel now
Days stood still; but blood will sting
Hand on the road you keep you in good stead
If you can feel the soul that remains
We pass on the road; you me and the shadows of life
Dreams of the past a milk float gone so fast
Passing is like the waking
A car passed within your passage
Time and pause the passage within your thoughts
Thoughts are a passage to the new world

Sold

I

The poor sit in there place,
With a sad face
Filling like a disgrace,
While the rich drink wine,
And fill there face,

II

Wasting food all over the place,
Which could help the poor man's fate,
No money no food end of another day,
Sleeping on the streets no were else to stay,

III

Swallowed pride as they beg to survive,
Their lives were sold to the bank on a loan,
But only a few enjoyed the money,
Destroying life saying the rest should pay,

IV

Streets are cold where life is sold!
People killed through a stroke of a pen,
Money never brought the seed to them,
Just lined the pockets of a few greedy men,
Sold their country on the blood of a wedding bed,

V

Promised the people their life's would change,
They would have freedom new chances to gain,
Everyone knew who would have to pay,
Banks will take their family in exchange,
Not from the ones who took the money and run,
But from those who lost their hopes and dreams.

Danger

I

Turn your eyes away from the scene,
As they tear down and sell the street,
Backhand police will never stop the thief,
Make up the figures with small time fish,
Sold by the ice cream man full of lies,

II

Smack-heads leaving needles at our feet,
Spreading diseases where our children play,
We have the power to end it today,
If only the police would come down of the fence,
Join the side they were formed to protect,

III

People say drugs are everywhere,
Think of our children as we offer this prey,
Cut out the cancer in which has grown,
In our society turning over our homes,

IV

Don't close your eyes pretend your blind?
Don't say you never saw the signs,
Funeral march on an aids ridden child,
Carry on with a turned face smile.

Reality

I

Laying on my bed full of dreams,
Twelve steps within the mind,
Reflecting the reality of the changing skies,
A changing man lying on these messed up sheets,
Feeling smashed out my head,
As the images dance on the edge of time,
Wondering why are these reflections dancing?
On the roof of the night in my mind,
Wondering if this is really a gun in my hand,
Feeling the cold metal of the edge of the stream,
Single drop slowly from my head
Falling down once more,
Upon this roller Costa of highs and lows

II

Falling through the paper ceilings of my mind,
So many levels to pass through,
When you are caught on a twelve month watch,
Seeing the stream of the river lights,
Never knowing or wanting this fall to seize
So many realities are shown on the dark side of the moon,
A home where you wish the journey will never end,

Chorus

Reality is just the door you open;
Stepping sometimes closer within your head,
Though you are faced with so many within your thoughts,
The light captured on the tears that you have seen,
The ones that have kept reality from your door,
Lost in a vacant space,
Caught within the echoes of the past,

Making you wondering what is the true reality?
The one that has captured you within so many rooms,

III

Left thinking; are the walls talking to me?
Who smashed the door on the second floor?
What are steps you hear within the night?
Waking in different beds of your life,
Lost in the reality that comes from all the lights,
Lost in the house that had been once green,
Who took the light from the walls?
Leaving me sitting in the corner all alone,
Feeling that little green men talking in my mind,
Wondering whose reality was really taken away?

IV

Monsters from the shadows of the night,
Have blinded the reality of my sight,
Left me on my bed spinning on a thread,
Flying high to the seventh step,
To meet the angel of death,
But he has nothing to take; not even my vest
Never knowing my mind had gone to war,
Am I just stuck in the reality of my bed?
Or stuck in the dreams held within my head?

Chorus

Reality is just the door you open;
Stepping sometimes closer within your head,
Though you are faced with so many within your thoughts,
The light captured on the tears that you have seen,
The ones that have kept reality from your door,
Lost in a vacant space,
Caught within the echoes of the past,

Making me wondering what is the true reality?
The one that has captured you within so many rooms,

V

Realities are the silent voices within twelve moons,
The ghost whispers caught in the sky,
The ones that reflect in the light of the darkness,
Dancing upon the images of the roofs in which we travel,
In the rapid flicker my soulless eyes,
A reflection of another world, space and time,
But the cold noise will keep your feet within this reality,
Knowing you will sit again within another wall,
The one that will reflect the moons of time,

VI

Reality of a sort; played like sport
Angels and devils playing in the universe of your soul,
Keeping you caught in the reality of life,
Ones that are shown within the lights of today,
You must decide which one's talk too fast?
Which ones hold the false illusion of reality?
Keeping up appearance in the false reality of today
Caught images in splinters of mirrors,
Reflects the true monsters within us all,
Turning quick from the reality,
That holds us within these different rooms;
Caught within so many paper walls; of the mind

Bad Thoughts

I

You set my heart on fire,
Destroying me with your lies,
Making love like a roller Costa ride,
That tight dress blows my mind,
When we fight I want to smack your face,
When you give head I know it's the best,
I see the danger in your shot up arms,
I know you're just a cheap porno star,

II

Eyes of brown words so unkind,
Lay on your back legs open wide,
Innovation for me to come inside,
Game of sex you should be knighted by now,

III

You think you know it all,
Wandering if I should stay or go?
When chasing the dragon giving head is all you know,
You have no pride when money you ride,
Fit one more up the rear,
Soixtante-Neuf is what you hold dear!

IV

Girls or boys you don't really care,
Strap on it's all the same fare,
It's about time you washed your greasy hair,
Spots on your face come in a different place,
Lowestoft air when legs are wide,

V

Down on all fours for a score,
All the way the pony way,
Snort snow white as you take seven up,
Knickers of white, yellow brown and red,
I know it's time to leave
But I think were already dead,
Then again it could be just bad thoughts.

Riddles in the Mind

I

Flying high in the sky,
Sniff the edge of the Milky Way,
Pupils open wide without a stare,
Will you take it all?
Or will you share,

II

Check your ticket on the line,
Marshmallow wheels on a car,
That doesn't want to drive,
Over mountains to the valley green,
Wear your high boots in the deep blue sea!

III

Take the girl in the black and white dress,
The one with the horses head,
What ever you need to make it through,
Your paying no matter what the point of view,
Burn the candle at both ends in your naked room,

IV

Demons talk in riddles and rhymes,
Sitting on a bean you've climbed,
Magic mushroom and jack your find,
Pigs in hats are waiting outside,
Talk in your mind not to noddy's friend.

Caverns

I

The boat still on the light,
Sipping from the light in streams,
Caught on the boat that moves nowhere,
In the stream on the horizon of time,
Dead in the sparks of life,
Caught in the caverns of rocks,
Blood bleeding within my head,

II

Caught on the cross that measures time,
On the ground; but caught in caverns of blood,
In a stream where heels never fall,
Where God has blinked in the mirror of the sky,
A boat that has stood still in the cavern of time,
Fingers deep within the blue sky,
Traces of hopes caught within the mind

III

Now God may be dead in water shallows,
The angels scream upon the waves,
As the hollow shatters and breaks within,
The cumbering rocks shatter on the shore,
The brain is split with endless moons,
The scares are far in moonlight skies,
On a boat in the caverns of the mind,
Caverns are shores within our thoughts,
Blood is the ocean of our hearts,

IV

Caverns may be a stream,
The wind and rain remain the same,
The thorns that bleed upon moonlight skies,
Are the which we die and never climb
The cavern reflects the mirror scream,
Walking in the hills; with blood on your hands,
Falling in the dark shadows of the mind,
We smile when we hit the sparkles of time,
We cry as the petals wash within our minds,
Now god and I may be caught in caverns
Searching for the vine that carries us through,
The stream below on ticks or snowball sky,
Tap, tip within the frozen mirrors of the sky

Meaning of Life

I

Exploring the meaning of life,
From the innocence of a child,
To the birth of a sacred smile,
Within ourselves an eternal journey,

II

All spinning upon the same wheel,
Back and forth on a tread mill of life,
Trying to find a meaning for it all,
When everyday everybody changes the rules,

III

A race against a mad hatter on a board,
On a throw of a dice wandering whom will fall,
Some will never leave the street, in which they are born,
While others will search within the skies,

IV

Exploring the meaning within our own time,
The changing season inside us all we all must find,
Of all the different meanings we were told as a child,
Stored on a journey within our mind,

V

Some of us will never wander why?
Or take the time to search inside our minds,
While others will spend a life time searching,
For the answer for which is burning,

VI

Maybe the answer is the question never there,
Then we have to wonder are we really here,
We've looked too hard for the meaning lost somewhere,
Inside us may be the only clue,
If there is a meaning to life or does life have no meaning.

Washed Upon the Waves!

I

The mind stands still in time!
The waves crash upon the rocks
Echoes of voices gone long ago!
The sea is a time within your soul
Your soul is the time you hold within
Gone are all the childish dreams
Lost in the space with no sunlight
Where are the demons you hold deep inside?

II

To catch the moon within your soul
To hold the light within your life!
Is to capture the light of God
To stand in the force of the love that remains
To claim you have served a better day
A naked person standing in the rain
Trying to stop the thoughts that keep me from going insane

Chorus

Waves clash upon an empty shore
Seagulls whisper the dreams you had
The sand, the plans you made
Washed out to sea in the timeless tides
How could you ever imagine a life of hope?
When the tides change in your seasons; like your mind

III

Time to watch the waves break and go
Time to watch the seasons within your mind
Time is a place; and place is a time
Standing still on the Yorkshire cliffs

As the waves crashed upon our feet
Mother; brother or father who kept our way!
To see the waves was to be part of life itself!

IV

Time will change on the ocean bound!
Waves of love and brothers never found
Repeats in our heart's in a distant crowd
Climbing the hill; but never too survive
Too reach the shores of brother's deep mind
Too stand in the coolest rain

Chorus

Waves clash upon an empty shore
Seagulls whisper the dreams you had
The sand, the plans you made
Washed out to sea in the timeless tides
How could you ever imagine a life of hope?
When the tides change in your seasons; like your mind

V

Time has changed and thoughts within my mind
Watching the sea disappear on the horizon
You held the dream; we held the hopes
That someday we could lift upon the waves
We stood in time; hearts clutching mine
Time is the past and time is mine
Upon the anchors they did shine
But to us they were passages of time

VI

A light on a moon light night
Changed your love and for me
Darkness came between you and me

Hate is the burning sea
The clear blue sea in which we never see
To torch a friend, a brother is all I see
But to torch my eyes
Within the lies you hide in disguise
Is to touch my soul and make all the waves cry in disguise

Chorus

Waves clash upon an empty shore
Seagulls whisper the dreams you had
The sand, the plans you made
Washed out to sea in the timeless tides
How could you ever imagine a life of hope?
When the tides change in your seasons; like your mind

VII

Violence upon silence
We acted upon life that never dreams!
We tore out the life that can never be seen
We took the life that you meant to me
You took my dreams; my reality
Lost like a ghost in my life
Like a child trying to find sunlight

VIII

"Maybe you never knew how much I love you!"
Maybe we will never meet upon n the street
It's a stare, a smile that keeps me alive
The waves will wash on the shore
The times collecting shell food on the floor
Will never take me back to the past
But in the stars I see
A vision of what could have been

Crystal Ball

I

Crystal ball in a rubber hall,
Bee that stings if you sing,
Sitting on a flower that will never seed,
So many cuts but did not bleed,

II

Anything seen in a band of gold,
How long has the factory been closed?
Frozen rose shattered in the snow,
Heart on a last petal sent,
Discarded with the rubbish on Wednesday night,

III

One night stand or twenty pound,
Like making love to the dead,
Thinking of the people who had gone long ago,
In a crystal ball of blood and tears,

IV

In a field of an abortion child,
Flesh and blood on someone else's name,
Dying rose tears could never revive,
Crystal ball smashed inside your head,

V

Time to walk on broken glass,
Now you've drunk from the chalices of poison wine,
Sold your soul on a cold bed,
If there is something left time to move on,
Poison wine on broken glass left me dead.

Another Time

Clocks ticking on the wall,
How far can you fly?
On a paper aeroplane in your mind,
How much honey can you take from the bees?
Walking backwards through the weeds,
Will you ever find the seed?
Do action men bleed when they're killed?
Do they make love to Cindy?
In the middle of the night,

II

All the kings' men will break down your door,
Don't be surprised
Watching like stars in the sky,
Who's watching whom on television screens?

III

Take it slow on a smoke,
Why rush when on the moon,
We all reach the same destination in the end,
Whisper words into an empty head,
One inside the strawberry jam jar,

IV

Forgotten things at the end of another war,
Who killed the dove of peace?
For the price of the licence fee,
We'll all to blame even me.

Stare into the Waters

I

Abyss heaven sent miss,
Wishing star seems so far,
Faithless touch in the middle of the night,
Ripples lost on a clear water still!

II

Blue moon on a faithless time,
Tender kiss on angels' wings,
Empty hall were we used to play,
Still chasing the bouncing ball,

III

Mist lost in the empty haze,
Broken tables chairs been cleared away,
Morning dew tempting brand new day,
You must decide whether it will be sun or rain,

IV

Play on the swings or build great things,
Did it pass you by in Tesco's line?
Searching in the abyss only you know what for,
But there's one thing we all need for sure,
A steady hand waters to bring a refreshing change.

Splinters in Thy Soul

I

Upon thy sword brothers blood wept tears,
Upon thy pen fear holds within,
Upon thy grave hence thee to the end,
Upon thy soul that grows far too old,

II

Words flow like wine at Virgins feast,
Harsh enough to spite the beast,
Gentle enough brushed upon a wish,
Told in lies when mixed with wine,

III

A song to dance upon dead feet,
Swift but slow light upon thy soul,
Words fall like dominoes in a row,
Crashing down in ones empty space,

IV

Left foot jester in a made up court,
Laugh on a wit far to short,
Deceitful juggler with no balls,
Fear within built on paper walls,
Torn down upon thy brothers sword.

Acting My Age

I

Acting Immature is all I want to do,
Reliving the child deep inside of me,
When I've only got one life to play,
I'll make up the rules day by day,

II

With all my ups and downs,
One day I'll play the clown,
Then I'll be as dark as a thundercloud,
When a man hides the child inside,

III

How can they expect a man to cry?
When as a boy, you're always told to smile,
To be a man on stubborn pride,
Never to show feelings inside,
Instead shed them through a childish smile,

IV

Then I'll keep on running around,
Never acting my age like you says,
When I'm only happy when I can play,
And I know I make you smile every single day,

V

Life's too short to even get you down,
Only you can age through a frown,
Then join the so-called respectable society,
The way in which children losing their identity,
But will you see the change in your face,
Will you miss all your childish grace?

Wondering

I

Taxis made out of stone,
Which sheep are the clones?
Sea air echoes the tune,
To the moors where they moan,

II

To the street full of holes,
Empty caravans fill the lanes,
Walking naked in the rain,
The worlds our own private plane,

III

We all look at each other,
Although deep down were all the same,
All born beneath the same sun,
Trying to capture life's sweet desire,
God knows how hard we have tried,
To keep up with the bills and comforts in life,
Like balancing an egg upon our foreheads,

IV

Walking through so many lines,
Bumping into so many rubber trees,
Hearing the sound of the mocking birds,
The trail of a man with different coloured skin,
Echoing the sounds of broken chains,
We wonder why things have never changed
As the big bad wolf keeps knocking on the door,
The white noise is burning into our minds,

V

We sit here wondering about our time,
Time we thought life were dreams and dreams were life,
Watching the years go by without a change,
Where we left our souls sitting on the shore,
Washed out to sea to be seen no more,
The case of wondering where life began
And where did we begin to hear the song.

Madhouse

A madhouse within silence and violence,
Voices chanting the haunting memories
Music playing with no chairs,
Echoes of days staring at the walls,
Age reflected in counting the days,
Bouncing yourself against a single wall,

II

Balancing on a three legged chair,
Wondering if you will stand or fall?
Out of fashion in bell bottom flairs,
In a house that has turned so many smiles,
Every day you pray for the madness to go away,
Told in plays and within school that everything comes within pairs,
Although you missed the steps upon the stairs,
Stumbled to the ground on shattered knees,
Knife in your arm; but the madness stays the same

Chorus:

Ball balancing, bouncing on a silent wall,
In line with your mind's eye,
Thoughts and dreams merge into the same,
Although always out a touch within your time,
As madness screams within the halls of your soul,
Which never ends till the ball hits the floor,

III

Stuck within the madness of your personal madhouse,
Not knowing what we wanted from life,
Crazy dreams wished upon a star,
The speech of the light shines within your soul,

A time that pauses within the house,
Never knowing if your dreams hold your slight delight

IV

Chasing the shadows within the darkened night
Like the blind who lead you from the fight,
Chasing vision the reflection in your mind,
Spinning on a stool, that is lost in time.

Chorus:

Ball balancing, bouncing on a silent wall,
In line with your mind's eye,
Thoughts and dreams merge into the same,
Although always out a touch within your time,
As madness screams within the halls of your soul,
Which never ends till the ball hits the floor,

V

Playing a piano with only one key,
Happy in my cod kipper shirt
Dancing in the corner; wearing no shoes,
In a mask within darkened spaces,
Tapping on the wall; thoughts of a secret code,
Hearing the sound of the past;
Displaying pictures within the mind,

VI

Caught within the sadness, madness within the home of the mind,
Stuttering, shaking, skipping through shadows of days,
The eye reflects the world upside down,
To the madhouse a cage we hold deep down inside,
Smile at the madness within your mind,
Flecks of which may never show within your time.

Questions in the mind

I

Room full faces staring from the pictures,
The sound of so many voices within your head
Wondering which blurred sound or face you can trust,
As I turn into the window screen of my life,
So many faces which make me run for the door,
So many lies within their fake smiles,
Making me want to escape from the madness,
Sit alone and stare at the shadows on the wall,
Questioning who can we trust in this life?
Who will see the real person within me?
Who will reach inside and pull me back to reality?
Who will ever answer the questions within my life?

II

Questions in the mind leave me sitting all alone,
In the corner of the hall; lost in dreams,
Watching the shapes and colours dance in the air,
A romantic dance on the walls,
Seeing the violence on the floor,
Feeling the blood drip in my mind,
Within the mind that has so many dark thoughts,
Shouting out questions in the silent night,
Trying to drown the screams in my head

III

Of all times sitting in my bed,
Pressed mental against my arms,
Watching the lights of light reflected within my hopes,
The shinning flash of the silver light,
Which cuts the hole in the parts of my mind?
A sense of liquid caught within the surface of grey,
What makes me question; why pain is such joy?

Feeling the liquid within my veins
Questioning have I always done my best?
Slipping through the shadows of the mind,
Within days with too many questions than answers,
Making me retreat within the shadows of the mind

IV

Though I must go to work to pay the bills,
Questions keep echoing in each step upon the streets
Why is my life this way?
Why do I keep walking in the reflections of my true self?
Never stepping away from the shadow of the past?
Why do I show too much of my feelings?
Lost in the rivers reflected in the moon shine,
Standing all alone within so questions,
Thoughts, hopes and dreams,
Of what I want to be and achieve,
Watching the flickers ripple within time,
Leaving me standing with questions within my mind,

V

Leaving me for days trapped within my bed,
Seeing visions within the flickers of life,
Watching the shooting dances on the edge,
The edge of the universe within a reflected mind,
Sparks dancing in the morning beam,
Stars of specks within a sudden stare,
Questions wondering why do I stay this way?
In a bed of blood and tears,
Believing the day I was born a cloud covered the sky,
Displacing the moon out of line,
Keeping me on the dark side of life,
Keeping me away from the light that holds so many dreams,
Questioning why would the spirits,
Always seem to keep me from the truth,

VI

Maybe it's the way my brain holds onto the past,
Reflecting the anger, betrayal and hate,
So many questions caught within a solid stare,
Showing a face of laughter and joy,
Question why do I try to fool the world,
The people around me who touch a shoulder cold,
Questioning why I laugh so loud,
Walking home all alone,
No steps of sounds beside me; or voices in my ears,
Feeling only the darkness in my life,

VII

Time leaves me questioning why I was born at all.
Maybe to show the darkness and strive within my life,
The light in the distant,
Hard to see in the crowds I surround myself within,
Questioning the choices I make to bring the light near,
Turning to see the dark side; in which I was born,
Caught on the edge staring down at the hole,
Feeling the light once within a moon,

VIII

I may never be able to explain these thoughts inside,
Knowing how I will explain what keeps me this way,
As the questions keep flooding inside,
Why I don't change!
So many questions within my mind,
People trying to pull me towards their light,
Moving away into the darkness of the night,
Lost in the demons that makes me feel safe,
Ones who whisper so much joy and pain,
Questions and answers that make me stand;
Lie in my bed or smile amongst the crowd,
Hearing the distant cries of the loneliness; I feel inside,

Keeps me alive and walking through the shadows of time,
Catching the different hands within my mind,

IX

How many times we question standing in a bar,
With closed faces that smile and talk too much,
Talk about you behind your back,
We must question the things we say to people,
Missed understood words or thoughts within my mind,
Makes me miss trust everyone I see,
Questioning why do I bother at all!
Just need to sit alone and watch and listen to the crowd,
The heard that think that they know it all,
Talking about people, life and choices,
Never really asking the big question within their lives,
Why do we all act and feel in different ways?
Maybe we are scared to face the crowd within ourselves!

X

So I turn with so many questions within my head,
Wondering if I will ever step across the void,
Take the time to find a different face,
To search so deep within my own,
Maybe too many scares are reflected in shadows?
Ones that hold so many demons and the joy,
Seeing the smiles of the dark eyes that reach,
Lost within the slight light within the darkness,
Knowing there is something I need to find,

XI

Seeing the beacon on the distant hill,
Questioning why I never leap to find,
Tapping the pebbles on the wall of time,
Hearing them fall in the cavern of my soul,
Smiling as each tear of a pebble drops,

Wondering and questioning why I enjoy the pain?
Why do I always see the darkness within the light?
Why do I never travel past the bridge lost long ago?

XII

Maybe I will travel across the shore,
Maybe the questions will give me the answers,
Knowing that more questions will take its place,
As I enjoy feeling the cuts on a body turned to stone,
Keeps the muse skipping in the reflected shadows of life!
Knowing this is part of my genes,
A family tree that can never see the trees,
So the light speaks to me and keeps me safe,
But the darkening questions fill me more with passion,
Makes me step within the willow trees,
To see what life I have to discover,
Leaving so many shadows behind,
Though more questions fill my mind,
On a blood filled trail that will never end.

Shatter:

I

Climbing up the chain of life,
Reaching for the hopes that I held within,
Pausing standing upon many shelves,
Looking over the horizon of time,
Setting the goals that keep us all moving forward,
Until a time we stop; pause and reflect,
Looking down within the void below,
Wondering if I fall from this height,
Will I smash on the ground and rise again,
A chance to walk and talk within life,

II

Standing upon the edge of the window frame,
Time makes you feel do you jump or stall?
What will you find in the darkness below?
Do you want to stand in the light behind?
Will I shatter on the rocks below?
Or climb to find a deeper meaning inside!
Find a new way within my life!
The steps that carry me back to a better place

III

We feel safe in the gardens of our hopes,
But to walk to the edge and shatter like a China doll,
Scares us from taking the risks that are deep within,
Taking the first steps to change our ways,
Built upon the safety that which enclose,
Though we need to jump many times from the bridge,
To shatter and rebuild ourselves within,

IV

Run to the anger that burns within our hearts,
To feel the lost and despair within our souls,
Time to stare within the words of the sun,
Feeling the silence within the days,
Knowing that we have to shatter on the shore,
To wake upon the waves that takes us out to sea,
So many times have the waves crashed down,
Turning my soul upon a different sand,
To hope that I will be stronger next time,
To shatter is to build upon a different land,

V

The steps across the sand,
Only leave the shattered dreams of yesterday,
The echoes and thoughts of so many footsteps,
The sand will change and the footsteps disappear,
Washed from the sands, through many memories,
The fall and shatter; still cuts deep inside,
How could we blame God; life or time?
We know the fall from grace will come like a speak,
A glance of the life you had before,
Standing on a factory floor,
Now I see a new of life,
But the shadows keep me falling on a shattered floor,

Chorus:

To shatter upon the wind,
Just like being caught within your dreams,
A day staring out at the world,
Caught within emotions and thoughts,
Feeling a new way within the streets,
As people turn and look at me,
Seeing a shattered; grown man within life,
As they pass along the grey cold streets,

VI

Taking a chance with ever card played upon a hand,
Moving along this passage of society and hopes,
Wondering which one will lead to my hopes,
Shattered many times of visions that showed a road,
The people who talked within my ear,
I can never listen to the voices caught in the night,
Telling and explaining what I should be!
I need to fall from the window,
Fall through the sky; feeling free,
Either to fly or shatter on the floor,
Pain of which will heal in time,
Scares on the brain keep me walking through empty streets,
Keeps me focused upon the hills, sky and light within,

VII

We are all shattered people,
Destroyed by the lies on the screen,
Keeps us pushing and shoving for the new technology,
Keeps us shattered within the thoughts of today,
As I still stand on the edge of the window,
Knowing I must fall,
To walk upon the horizon of my mind,
A reflected time and a place we are scared,
To walk through so many mirrors of time,
To shatter upon a diamond drop,

Chorus:

To shatter upon the wind,
Just like being caught within your dreams,
A day staring out at the world,
Caught within emotions and thoughts,
Feeling a new way within the streets,
As people turn and look at me,

Seeing a shattered; grown man within life,
As they pass along the grey cold streets,

VIII

So I fall from this window once again,
Feeling the breeze and thrill of life,
Breaking through so many walls and times,
Falling through so many stars,
Crashing and shattering on the ground below,
Standing tall when life had nothing for me,
Still standing on the edge of the window frame,
Waiting to jump once more,
Feeling the freedom of air,
Seeing my green eyes shatter then form once more,
Knowing that there was a cloud that I have fallen from,
I never falling from the shatters of my dreams,
Until I feel the last breathe within my soul

Why Do these Things
Happen to Me?

I

I'm sitting in a dark room,
The shinning blade,
Moves across the stars,
That drifts in the hollow sky of the night,
Mixed with the blue and red,
As my arms sting in the fluid of my thoughts,
Wondering how and why you make me feel this pain!

II

Shadows hang the loss on the wall,
Never wanting to walk school,
Hearing the beats within the street,
Washed up eyes within the rain,
Hanging on the slab upon yellow lights,
Will you care to see the silhouette?

III

Your taunts and bruises
Have left me stuck in the corner!
Shivering through the light of life
All I wanted was to chase the dreams in streams,
You took the clouds and kept demons within,
Walking through alleys of life,
Cutting the stream; within my eyes,
Walking through ghosts; holding time,
Something I thought I held in my mind,

IV

You have taken the roads and senses,
Ones I held in the shallows of mind,

Left me in darkness of the snow
With a trail of red in the pure right,
Wondering why?
You should me feel this way!
Why do you skip through in puddles this way?

V

Sitting in chair blinded by the screen,
Talking through the windows!
Hanging on the words and threats,
Bullies scare me within Sunday's wash,
Keep me chasing visions stalled upon the walls,

VI

Now it's me standing on the chair,
Will you care in the silent breeze?
Snap; is the breeze that set me free!
No more hurt in the green trees!
No more steps in the puddles of life,
You are the bully, who has taken,
So many eyes and steps within my thoughts

VII

Swinging in the cool breeze!
Clouds as I'm talking to you?
From beyond the moon,
Dolphins jump and dance in the sky
Silk is skin on the beginning
Inner demons turn you round
To the bullies; that holds our lives!
Never feeling the silk within my dreams,
Holding close the chances in night
Darkness is the light in which I tread,

VIII

Now the skin has gone,
Hanging in the yellow light!
Do you care for the light that once sparkled?
That danced on the edge of life
Now hung underneath the waters of time,
Looking through the bubbles of my mind,
To see a man standing; with no time,

IX

You bullies hide and cry!
In streets that you will never climbed!
Left me standing on a smashed glass in life!
Cutting my arms or my mind!
Laughing as the liquid fills the sky
You pushed me to the edge of my brain!

X

Now I'm travelling through the stream
No motion of up or down,
In school they told you I hung from the sky!
On weekend loose in a darkened room!
Now the bullies see the flash
Sparks in the night
An image caught in the day break light!

XI

But my grave will remain my bed,
I died in '89
Crashing heads of bullies inside,
Dead on a stool caught in your head!
Bullies in my life!
Had me turn and face the shallow shores,

Now this loose hangs in moon list sky
As I smile as I jump from the frame

XII

You are the bullies
That shattered all my nights,
How do you feel know?
Watching my body dancing,
In the stillness of the night sky,
With hopes and desires,
No longer counting the graves,
Blood flows in a single stream,
I'm drowned in these thoughts,
Fish upside down within the stream,
Knowing my brain is already dead,
The bullies pushed me the edge,
Know I'm caught within life and death!

XIII

Taking the knife on a motionless sky
The bullies caught forever within my head,
Cutting in my veins,
As the shinning side,
Starts to climb
I as you the question why?
Does my life mean nothing to you?
As I climb to the mountains high!

XIV

The tear will only fall in families eyes
the steps they take on a grey day!
Echoes I wish shatter your ears,
As the heavens cry down from the sky
Asking the question "How can you take a mind?"

XV

Now you must reflect on your actions?
How could you drive a spirit into the darkness?
How did your words swing within the clouds?
Do you now feel safe in the corner of the room?
When you broke the seventh seal of life!
You took a young person to the grave within,
Held him down with stares and broken lies,
Knowing one day you must face a light
Caught down within all our bodies and souls,

XVI

Now the bullies and me
Are caught walking upon the seventh step
Caught in time on a screen of our mind,
Trickles fade; but passages never die!
Through all of time the question remains the same!
Why do you do these things happen to me?

THE FEATHER OF THE NIGHT THAT ONCE TOUCHED WITHIN:

Cutting Edge

I

Your deep Ocean eyes,
Make me feel like I fly to the edge,
Of the world; to stare upon the shores,
Ones that keep the crashing waves,
From the edge of the madness I hide inside,
Of all the times I swam out too far within the sea,
Seeing your eyes reflected on the horizon,

II

You green eyes make me drift in the universe of time,
As the world spins around the tomb of the waves,
Keeping me struggling on the tide of the edge,
Treading the waters within my mind,
Feeling the swirl upon my frozen feet,
Carrying me to tomorrow,
Stuck in the sands of the past,

III

Offering up my shattered heart,
To the moon that reflects so many lost times,
Like a piece of pie on the edge,
Maybe for a friends or passing stranger,
Feeling the knife cut so deep within me,
Spilling the blood within the crashing waves,
Feeling myself on the stream of life,
Caught within the cutting edge of my skin,
Feeling the lies told you and me,

IV

We skim across the edge of the waters,
Hiding so much love inside,

Never searching under the white waves,
That carries us to the bitter sun,
We know there is so much love inside,
Though we laugh through the tears of the night,
As we hide all the thoughts and feelings inside,
Wearing a clowns disguise; within the clouds,
Knowing they have two sides to walk within your life,
Though we know we must this disguise in time,
When you are always caught on the edge,
Seeing faces pass in these happy filled London streets,

V

So we step naked in the water of the mind,
Reaching for the light within the sky,
Pausing still; upon a blood filled mile,
Knowing there is nowhere to run or hide,
Feeling the beat of the heart upon one line,
Feeling the highs and lows of a cutting edge,
Stepping across the bodies left within the shore,
So many ghost of the past,
Your faces show so many times on the world,
The cutting edge which made me feels insane,
Where you drowned on a bitter stream,

VI

So much fun reflected upon the cutting edge,
The red water is breeze within my stream,
On the fun we see flashing in the lights,
The desire and lost in the cold blue moonlight,
We travel through the mirrors of time,
The flashing blue lights keep us walking on the edge,
The cutting edge lost in shadows of time,
With blood around us on the ground,

VII

Now you see through my cutting eyes,
Seeing the emptiness I hold so deep within side,
Turning like the tide on a pacific green,
As the storm warns us of such deserter
Watching you walk tall upon the shore,
Leaving me in the shallow waters of today,
Your steps are drowned by my own thoughts,
Keeping me on the cutting edge,
Tearing like wolves at my heart soul,
Knowing the edge is the place I want to be

Look in your eyes

I

I have seen your changing eyes,
Within the drops of footsteps in the ground,
Turned from walking in the light of day,
To standing in the shadows of your open eyes,
The ones that used to look beyond the clouds,
Seeing there was more to me; than just a figure,
A shadow reflected on the wall moons,
Chasing shadows in the shutters of the garage doors,

II

We stepped across the many graves within our time,
Chasing the ghost that said we should stop,
Followed by the cross of time,
Running; chasing our eyes within youthful dreams,
To a time when we faced our open grave,
Looking into your eyes that burn in the night,
Light a fire that glows in heaven,
Turning to see the emptiness within mine,
Only pleasure and pain may glow,
In my eyes; wanting the desire in your eyes,

III

I felt you walked into the darkness,
Though the look the look in your eyes,
Showed me you stepped into the light
Through my fingers that only held the dark side,
A place with only demons and screams,
Knowing I was to blame for look in your eyes,
Testing your love more and every day,
A silly game like drafts or chess in a club of dreams,
Smiling as I change within the lights,
Losing the changing look within your eyes,

IV

Knowing I'm the one to blame,
Testing you every day,
Turning in the stare on the dance floor,
Tiny steps to choose what's right,
Seeing so many eyes within my mind,
Silly games played upon the steps of time,
Leaving me staring at the eyes that have turned,
Bored with the darkness I hold inside,
Making me feel so much pain,
On the cutting edge of desire,

V

Save from my inner self,
The destruction that keeps me from your eyes,
When I enjoy all the emptiness inside myself,
Keep looking in the darkness within me,
Feeling safe within the emptiness of my soul,
Looking in your eyes but only see darkness,
Wanting to feel your shelter,
The hope of life and dreams,
A long road within the mountains,
In which we climb to find the sun and moon,
Twelve times within the sky,

VI

Sitting in the room of flashing hopes,
On the waters screen that flash in the mind,
Tapping, skipping on the streams of time,
Seeing the look within your eyes,
You wanted more than life that I could bring,
Seeing the look change to a different scene,
Leaving me standing in a pool so cold,

VII

Wondering why I tested you every day,
Pushing you to edge of the time,
The one caught between our desires and love,
Sheets are same and blood remains,
Staring in the mirror of the toilet walls
Smashing the eyes that stare from behind,
Feeling the pain within the look of your eyes,
Knowing the joy I feel within the pain,
It keeps me falling over the edge,
The void which has been there from birth,
Knowing I will never capture within the eyes,
Of the ones who show that life has a reality,
A voice screaming in the night,
Death of a thought within the mind,

VIII

So many eyes in the sheets of the voids,
To look within the eyes in the chambers of the mind,
To open the closet that screams full of pain,
Lock the door and stare at the closed filled eyes,
Walk upon the hills that never show emotion,
Never turning back when I carry the load upon me,
My shoulders burn and my eyes are blood red,

IX

Pausing; turning to see the light within your eyes,
I wish I could step within those golden eyes,
But to me life is one of lose and despair,
I love to see the wooden stakes and the blood within our minds,
Though to look in your eyes is a dream,
A stream that cleanse even the bitterest soul,
But I must turn and follow the wolves in the night,

X

I never want to destroy the look in your eyes,
It's just a warning to never step upon the trail I walk,
Steps I take every day,
Between the light and moon,
Seeing the destruction within the world,
Never wanting to this destruction within your eyes,
Your look within eyes those are pure,
Can only be destroyed by the darks eyes of mine,
I wish I could walk upon your eyes of dreams,
Knowing I would only shatter your hopes and dreams,
When all I see is the darkest of the night,
Mixed within blood of the eyes,

XI

Now we walk upon the clouds of night,
You see the sun; I see the rain,
The look of your eyes makes me fall in the graveyard,
Stopping; standing in the coldness of my mind,
Reaching up; but never wanting to feel your hand,
Scared I will pull you down into this dark side,
Wanting only to want that look in your eyes,
The one that said I was more than a man,
Keeps me skipping from the grave,
As the blood trickles from my eyes,
Unto a lonely ground on the mountain
Days focusing the look within your eyes

Precious One

I

I've made all kinds of crazy plans,
Moved the post to shoot for goal,
There were even times I stole,
Now you've changed the nature of the game,
Some crazy times will remain,
But my thoughts will never be the same,
Then again that's not a bad thing,
When I can see a new meaning on the screen,

II

You've become the air I breathe,
My million to one lotto win,
Your mum and me couldn't work out our thing,
Push comes to shove you were made out of love,

III

I'll never regret a single day,
When I am blessed with you,
Now you've shown me a different way,
Even though I'm the one who has to be strong,
My tiny bundle I can't wait for you to come,
You're my life, my love, my precious one.

Things to Say!

I

There are so many things,
I want to say
Tried to call you today,
Choking on stupid pride,
Still feeling you by my side,
Breathe upon my neck,
Fingers running down my spine,
Turn around to find you're not there,

II

Remember making love in the car,
We swore we would never
Let one another go,
Not just words in the heat of the night,
You took my words before they were said,

III

You walked away I must have been blind,
Every time we meet I trip on my own pride,
Counting days when you were last at my side,
Happiness in memories is all I can find.

Time After Time

I

Some things are for the best,
Even though you don't know it yet,
Losing your job to losing your way,
Time to time we all stray,

II

Different ways opportunity knocks on your door,
It might not come your way today,
These are times we have to be strong,
Their come a time when you know you belong,

III

We all have a different plan,
We all hear a different song,
Friends will always help us through,
Maybe even a partner or two,

IV

Different times means different roads,
Time after time challenge is unknown,
Take my hand as we hop from stone to stone,
We may fall in the waters cold,
Maybe for the best to find our pot of gold,
Togetherness will always help us win.

English Rose

I

A single red rose,
Just to let you know,
I still care
Friendship will always be there,
Rose will never wither or die,
Petals never had time to fly,
Thorns will never cut inside,
When love never had time to grow,

II

It brought blood to my empty veins,
Desert quenched by rain,
Green eyes no battle there,
Brown eyes have showed so much care,

III

My English rose
Through you so many things have grown,
You showed me how to be a real man,
My heart will always be your rose.

Famous Last Words

I

In the letter you wrote,
One you forgot to post,
Flowers that were never sent,
Pictures on an empty mirror frame,

II

Cold in a blue filled room,
On a chair in a field going nowhere,
Room or field which ones really there,
Bluest skies letters everywhere,

III

Double Dutch or just too much,
Standing still or spinning on a wheel,
Words echoing in our minds,
Sound of footsteps on the stairs,

IV

Burning bridges in the midnight hour,
On a train with no driver,
Lost in a burning fire
Wishing to extinguish the letters of the past,

V

Waiting in holding baggage class,
Stuck in a cubical lost and found,
Words to find I know I should have tried,
Famous last words always end in goodbye.

Babe

I

I've sung the blues for so long,
Trying to find the time
Searching for something special,
Caught always staring out the door,
You showed me how too look within,
To find myself beyond the clouds,
You gave me the strength to carry on,
To look forward to the days that remain!

II

I didn't ask were you come from,
I just know were you belong,
In my heart lost in a distant song,
The one I've been searching for so long,

III

You brought the sun to darkest clouds,
Lighting up my life something not felt before,
Special kind of drug to make me feel high,
Harsh words will always make me cry,

IV

But I'd always return to your tender love,
Your loves the fix in which I need,
Without it my heart will surely bleed,
After you showed me there's much more to me,

You showed me love when I was on the empty sign,
Step out the door and showed me what to find,
Sometimes the world can be so kind,
But it's only your love that can make me feel this way,
End of the day you're my special babe.

Ray of Hope

I

You look at me as if you don't know me,
As if love we never shared,
Maybe you just don't want to know,
Problem I guess only you can solve,

II

Look as hard as your words,
First time in my life I no longer feel low,
State of the world still makes me mad,
But my child makes me glad to be alive,

III

I hope one day I'll find true love,
One day the world will be a better place,
Now content to walk at a slower pace,
But still to have a few moody days,

IV

But not to darken up my life,
Now I'm content, with whom I am,
No longer feeling second best,
A ray of hope on a different light.

Strong

I

Picture seemed to blur,
Out of focus always looking the wrong way,
Upside down or was life back to front,
When you feel like it's cut you inside out,

II

On your own kicking a stone,
Echoes in the night voices asking who's right,
Don't judge the past on miss heard rumours,
All I know is its time to do the right thing,

III

Back in line strong in focus of mind,
Real father stands while others run with lies,
A promise to never leave your side,
For you're in my heart till the end of time,

IV

Direction in which never to stray,
Guiding hand always to be there,
When everything I do is for you,
Stand in life to become a real man,

V

Though some may class me as a rolling stone,
Lost in words on miss direction, promises and dreams,
You brought the wind to my broken wings,
Showed me how to be strong,
Brought me the light to help me see,
Given me a reason in which to believe?

On My Mind

I

I can't get you of my mind,
No matter how much I try,
Wondering if you put a spell on me,
When will I see you again?
I feel like a child of ten,
I try to keep myself occupied,
Changing the wheels of my mind,
In the memories is where you hide,
The ones I keep recalling every time,
Your smiling face burned within my mind,

II

Though we don't know each other that well,
I know there's so much I want to say,
But the words don't seem to come out right,
Until I see your face and warm smiles,
To see your face the glow of which
I would travel a lifetime to see,

III

I feel your close in the picture in my mind,
Even when we are miles apart,
From the time I go to bed,
To the time I raise my head,
A magical time spent were you heaven sent,

IV

From the corner of the room,
To the back of my mind,
I can't stop thinking about you,
You're all I need to get by.

Blind

I

Looking for gold in a mountain of coal,
No weight of diamonds could fill the hole,
When all that glitters is never what it seems,
In this world people can be quit mean,

II

Everybody's looking for perfection in every way,
But when blind how are you going to see,
Trying to change the person inside of me,
Change me to someone I don't want to be,

III

Treating me like a second class citizen,
How much money do I have to bleed?
If only I knew your heart was full of greed,
Like some of your friends when money is what you feed,

IV

You laugh at me when I say I still feel real,
I open my heart to show you how I feel,
You left a mark as you walked through without a care,
When the money was gone you were no longer there,
You must have caught me in a blind stare.

Angel Sent

I

Lord I've prayed for an angel,
Every single night and day,
I hope you send her my way,
To heal this pain I feel,

II

I've searched all round this town,
I've even been down on my knees,
But all I feel is pain and misery,
As I end everyday as lonely as can be,

III

Oh lord, oh lord I pray and cry every day,
For someone to come and rescue me,
To dry my wells I call eyes,
To hold all the love I have inside,

IV

I know your send an angel of mine,
But it's hard in these lonely times,
To keep the faith and peace of mind,
When every day I seem to fall further behind,

V

I search every day for this angel of mine,
Maybe I'll have to travel to different town,
For the love of joy I search for all around,
Show me the light please don't leave it too late,
I promise I'll love her till the end of time.

Love in the Past

I

We met in a middle of a disco tech,
We may have been young,
But we knew love when our eyes met,
Everyone said it was puppy love and would not last,

II

But just that stare will stay
With me till the day I die,
And the feeling in which we search for every day,
Fumbling in the dark, searching for the words to say,
First slow dance you pray will last forever,

III

Holding her body tight
Holding her body close,
Moving your feet just going with the flow,
Emotions running as your hands tremble,
Not knowing if they're going too far,

IV

Skin so smooth as you hold her so tight,
Thinking we can stay like this till the end of time,
In one night you find and lose your heart,
Now all you can do is hang it on the line,

V

From the time your lips touched mine,
I felt like I was on cloud nine,
Now I'm forever trapped within lover's eyes,
My heart is under a magical smile.

Blind to See

I

I've stopped on the road,
Watching your lights fade into the dark,
Leaving me all alone and cold,
Sending my heart to stone,
They say that true love is blind,
So why can't I find,
The love to carry me on through,
When I'm too blind to see,
The love that's in front of me,

II

But all I see is the past,
Instead of living in the present time,
Staring in the mirror at what I left behind,
Caught in days leaving me so blind,

III

Never seeing the bright lights of true love,
Even when they're on the highest beam,
When your blind to all you see,
And love becomes a distant memory.

Shopping

I

Checkout on an empty shelve,
Maybe it's the way I'm dressed,
On a ticket for sale or return,
But my hearts already been burnt,
In between calls on the phone,
Buried like a long lost bone,
Life's a shopping trolley going nowhere,
Sold down the river, just give it time,

II

Hopscotch landing were you've been before,
Same old faces on a shopping trip,
The shop they say only fools rush in,
But now it feels too much like home,

III

Sit on the shelve and take a last wish,
All on sale for everything's cheap,
Down a scotch or slash your wrist,
Either ways a step closer to the pit,

IV

Tear in your eye,
On a laugh and a smile,
Don't let them know they've won,
They say one-day love will come,
On the street or maybe on a shopping trip.

Green Eyed Monster

I

The first thing you want to know,
Not what is my star sign!
But how much money do I earn,
What's the style of car do I drive,
I think it's just the beer I hear,
As I see the pound sign in your eyes,
Something I missed in that first stare,
I don't know what more you can take from me,

II

You say I'm a dreamer with my head in the clouds,
You say that money makes the world go round,
But I always thought that was love?
Maybe that's why you see everything as a pound sign,
Everyone just an investment in time,

III

Your turned on by the braggers on money talk,
On a bank balance your knickers come down,
Money can't buy love words you've never heard,
For money is the only love your heart knows,
Monster with green eyes full of greed

Connection

I

Feeling the connection has gone,
Bond of which made us strong,
Thought you were the song within my trees,
Thing to unlock my lost memory,

II

Silver and gold lost in a day,
Steel of blade blinded in the sun,
Caesar of seven but only took one,
Blood that spilled onto an empty stone,

III

Pulled into mist covering my head,
Moister of rain stinging my face,
Lost in fog carried inside of me,
Only I can dispel if I could find the spell,

IV

But the lines always feels engaged,
Glimmer of hope on a love of want,
All in the mind on a child left behind,
Slap in the face when you try to understand why,

V

Stutter in time as days roll on by,
Too long now to ever return to lovers kiss,
Walls too high to ever climb inside,
Broken down line connection gone for all time.

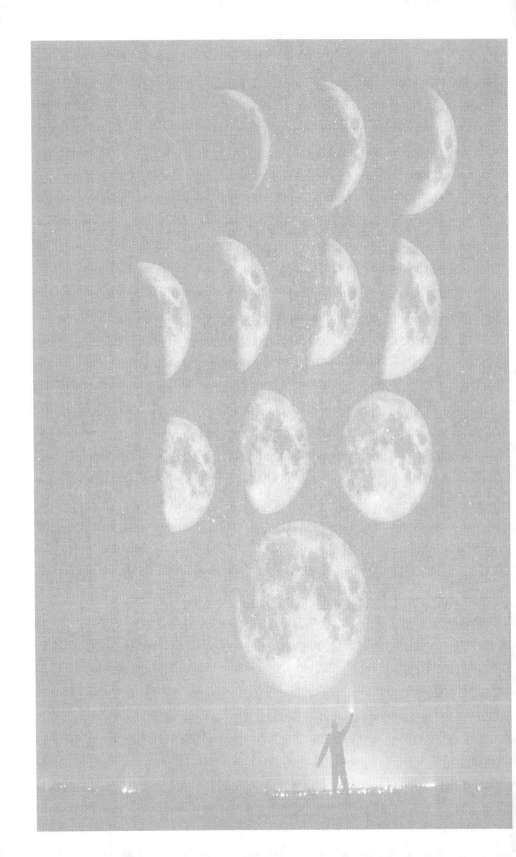

CHANGING MOODS WITHIN TWELVE MOONS:

Laughter Time

I

Clocks starts to unwind,
Time passes with the blind,
Flash of moment in my mind,
Laughter to times I cried,

II

Words jumbled on a board,
Find the right ones if I could only try,
You look at me as if I've lost my mind,
You're properly right: I'm a looking glass,
If only life was that kind,

III

Silent pause banging of doors,
To the sound of a silent scream,
What's the time; panic in your eyes,
Move away try to show a nice smile,

IV

Nights like this wondering should I pay,
Indiscreet moment in the hay,
But to call I'm too shy,
So I'll stand here and wait for another try,

V

But the clocks saying please be quick,
Late like the rabbit for the mad hatter,
Now I'm grey and it doesn't matter,
Times gone on a single laughter,
I wonder if I really could have found her.

Excusses

I

Burning bridges on plastic cars,
Never seem to travel far,
10p short of the single fare,
Working to pay the shoe repair,

II

Feet are flat nose is red,
Things never done excuses for each one,
I could have travelled to the moon,
If only I had the time
Which passed too soon!

III

Blooded knees on thorny hills,
Give it one more week and I'll leave,
Once I've paid the credit card on a big wheel,
Round and round in circles,
Balancing on a jelly bean,

IV

Now I'm too old to go,
I must keep up the race,
For the things for the home,
Now I'm just one of the clones.

Maybe Tomorrow!

I

Every year passes the same,
Like I'm in a rut in these clouds,
Following the darkness of the sky,
Walking each day to an empty sound,
Searching everywhere within the crowd,
Lost on the footsteps of life and time,
Stuck in a crowd; but nowhere to be found,
Growing; trying to find the meaning,
Lost somewhere on the rolling hills of time,

II

Maybe tomorrow I'll find the spark,
Caught within the light deep inside of me,
Till then I'll sit and look at the changing moons,
Twelve within a paper sky,
Seeing the tears and feeling the scars,
As the hope reflects within my dreams,

III

Thinking back to the child standing still,
Caught within so many clouds,
Wondering through the halls of school,
Never finding the words on the walls,
As the darkness filled my mind,
Feeling it was all just a waste of time,
Missing the words that echoed in the halls,

IV

Time is a memory which we can change,
When we are always caught in a rut,
Looking for a new avenue to walk upon,

Wishing I had stopped and listened,
To the words spoken at the back of the hall,
Feeling the fear to step across the middle line,
To try and fall upon the paper within,
To search for the thoughts and memories,
To reason why I have stayed upon this street,
One that holds no pathway in life,

V

Turning to feel the cold block of the brick,
Knowing I can only walk forward,
Feeling a burning knowledge or desire deep within,
Wondering when I will turn the corner,
To see a different place,
A different man in the yellow street lights,
Maybe I will give time,

VI

In my mind images of the past flash,
A silhouette of a figure standing in a line,
On a production line in a hazy dream,
Working in the list of factories and the street
Feeling the last coins at the end of the week,
Always saying maybe tomorrow,
Will be a start of a different day,

VII

Passing by the broken; boarded houses,
Chimneys broken on the estate of hate,
Eyes and heads walk slowly in the sky,
Making me sit on the edge of it all,
As the violence screams from the window panes
Trapped within the drops that never stops falling,
Making us believe; maybe tomorrow,
We will shake off these demons inside,
Free our heads of all the different lies,

VIII

So I turn; still sitting on the edge,
Thinking tomorrow will come in my bed,
To hold the flame of the candle within,
Maybe tomorrow I will build the single stone,
To hold the block that swells inside us all,
To keep the faith when we stand in the rain,
To step across the line,
Holding life deep inside,
To never feel the rut within the stream,
To chase the moons within the skies,
Maybe tomorrow I will see a better day

Decision Time

Decisions to be made,
Should I stay and fight,
Should I leave like a thief in the night?
Now I have no more cards left in my hand,
You won't see me here again,
Held back for far too long,
In a cellar told not to run,
Watch the changing seasons of the sun,

II

Wondering if I want to break free,
From the chains only I can see,
Decisions did I leave my precious one,
Regret of which to haunt me throughout my life,

III

Though I know I must go,
Problem is I'll never see you grow,
But to fly I had to try,
I hope your understand it just takes time,
On the wind the message you will hear,
Daddy loves you and was never that far,
I'll hold you in my heart till the day I die.

Drowned

I

Tied to the front of a ship,
Drowned in oceans like a figure head,
Up and down in oceans cold,
A slave that was never sold,
Tempted by the devils hand,
All for the sake of a pile of coins,
What would we find?
If we turned the world upside down,
This is no way to treat mankind,

II

Mists rolled in were devils played,
Injustices sought on a forgotten town,
Burn the schools and houses the same,
Do you feel the weight of the chains?
Are we all rolling further down the drain?

III

On a train whose driver is blind,
In a tunnel would we know if the sewers explode?
Are we blind to the crap about town?
In the words too many times have we drowned?
Sell our souls theirs nothing else around,
We made our planet our personal grave.

Hole

I

Hole in my jumper,
Missing puzzle in life,
Face blurred on a paper trace,
Shot before the race,

II

Lemon bitter and sweet,
Egg and chips on a coffee week,
Hole in your shoe no sign of snow,
Knocking on the door with no where to go,

III

Glass of milk for everyone you meet,
Enchant mousier are words that greet,
Picture puzzle different things are seen,
A piece of peace when eyes are clean,

IV

Pinhole in a picture blue,
Apple land if you look through,
Echoing all you take is you,
Naked as everyone we all have the missing piece,
Join together to fill the hole within

Broken English

I

In broken English you spoke to me,
A distant dream lost somewhere in my mind,
Then you told me your name is dream,
Not knowing you're the girl I've always seen,
As you become more than a dream should mean,

II

Lost so deep within your eyes,
As your smile brings the waters to my shore,
Seeing your eyes in a distant fire,
On the waves I feel your tender smile,

III

I will travel through time and space,
From the desert sands to the coldness of the snow,
Over hilltops within my mind,
Just to fall at your feet and hold you inside,

IV

When your love is the only food I need,
Quenching my thirst with a single kiss,
Easing my pain with the slightest touch of your hand,
Taking me away within your tender breath,
As I sink further into your arms,
I know that paradise will call me this time,
A pleasure of love and life,
That will remain within me throughout my life,

V

So in broken English talk to me,
Your voice whispers in my ears,
Even when you are not so near,
Your tender breeze caught within my soul,
Tells me there is a place called home,
No more footsteps caught within the heavy snow,
As my soul warms with loves sweet desire.

Silent Flute

I

A silent flute carried upon the night,
A distant sound beneath the sand,
Free travelling with voices on the ground,
Mixing with all the different desert sounds,
From when the sun has laid to rest,
Though some might believe it's dead,
Until again it raises its head,
When they say we are born upon the sun,

II

Then the flute may play for you,
If you listen to its magical tune,
Your hear the silent voices carried there,
On the desert in which you stare,

III

Carried on a Valuker of waters still,
As the voices whisper beneath the sails,
A magical flute as the water never makes a sound,
Caught in the rapids so strong,

IV

Never moving as the water rocks you back and forth,
In the night until you hear the silent words from within,
Of the silent flute as your heart carries the tune,
One of a kind till you find peace of mind.

Day Party
(Enjoy Yourself)

I

Spread your wings upon seven seas,
If only in a dream
Taste the sun and girls one by one,
Swim in seas have some fun,

II

Remember the times when you were young,
Release the child we all hold inside,
Taste from the cup we call life,
In any way that turns you on,

III

Exotic waterfall made for two,
More than one way to enjoy a pleasure ride,
In a group if you enjoy the show,
Life's a party all you have to do is go,

IV

Don't be put of by anyone,
We all have wings to touch the sky,
Don't wait for the weekend to have some fun,
Everyday you're own party only you know how to play,
So spread your wings and enjoy every day.

One Fine Day
(Take The Blame)

I

Yesterday seems a long time ago,
Tomorrow will come too soon,
Leaving me alone in the afternoon,
Time with memories to burn,
For all those days I'll take the blame,
You say I brought you down,
I brought the rain
Something we've all felt before,

II

Friends will move to the sound
Of the division bell,
Talk in anger when words of love
Are hard to tell,
Under broken arrows were we fell,
For yesterdays rain I'll take the blame,

III

Let the light dance shadows into today,
Angels and devils they all look the same,
When you're caught between the sun and rain,
Waiting for one fine day,

IV

Carry the cross until that time,
When you won't share the blame,
So I'll stumble and burn in the flame,
One-day love will fall like holy rain,
A guiding hand will help me stand.

Take Five

I

Take five from saving the world,
Worrying about the pending dust clouds,
One day the sun may explode,
Why worry so many things to kill you anyway,

II

Lets take a ride on a miss hype,
Take a chance backward falling on a slide,
Swim naked across the Tyne,
Lay in your lap watch the stars in the sky,

III

I sometimes worry too much about the world,
To a point were I can no longer see,
Night of laughs to argue the point I believe,
Sometimes happiness is the language I need to find,

IV

Standing upon my soap box pedestal,
Like I have done many times before,
Preacher man a gospel to be sung,
Idealistic ideals to free mankind,

V

No man is ever to be my king,
When a king is only a man,
No reason to bow and kiss upon a hand,
But take five and have a night of wild mind,

VI

For it's hard to change the world overnight,
Sometimes all you need is the touch of a gentle hand,
Take your time to walk along country bends,
Take five to spend time with special friends.

Scrutinize
(Question and Answers in Life)

QUESTION:

I

What are you searching for?
In this place of the blurry eyed,
Something for the night or a weekend delight,
Do you know or do you look much further,

II

Like an astronomer searching for a new star,
Explorer searching for something new,
Scientist searching foe the right key,
A writer trying to write the right play,

III

Do you want just a fumble in the night?
Would it be too hard to say this was right?
Your eyes show that you would care,
As you ask me is love fair,

IV

But love is rare when sex is everywhere,
The light you seek sometimes seems so bleak,
Tears of rain will never touch your feet,
Hearts of gold on devils lips are sold,

V

Locked inside all the words you want to cry,
In your head, in your bed your heart you tried to hide,

On a dream in a stream or so it seems,
Is she tall, is she small you have to tell me,

ANSWER:

VI

Waiting for the girl to take my hand and understand,
Touch each others hearts that beat so fast,
On a trembling kiss to re-light my soul,
Open my mind becoming my special key,

VII

Turn of a lock blind now I can see!
Show me loves not just a thing on the screen,
Made up by fools and those of us who believe,
In eyes of smiles we were never born to be one,
I don't believe that love has gone,
In this world I'll search till I find that girl,

VIII

To care for me not the pretty green,
To hold me tight on a cold rainy night,
To wish for me like I wish for her,
Cuddle each other tight on a last piece of coal,

IX

Big or small love is within,
Eyes of souls which never hide,
Walk in the sun child may come,
Talk for hours letting each other inside,

X

Fight now and then but love will never die,
Tender rose to hold through out the night,
That part of me to make me feel right,
The one to fill the hole in one,
Unite as one to unlock the sun,
So I'm searching for my unplanned song.

Twelve moons

I

A Hollywood play; nightmare within a day
A familiar script driven upon a wish
Gone so fast in the moons of time
Twelve moons reflect within your mind,
Time stood still on the clouded street;
Heart will skip or turn to stone
Funny how the calendar will fly with time

II

A birth stone washed upon your hands
A distant kiss upon the silent trees at night
In the air; with no more disguises
The sun will chase the rain clouds away,
Although the moon will spin and dance in your mind
To the childish dreams; long lost ago
To the time you spent watching every one go
The moons will shine within your mind;
Time will past like a hawk within the night

Chorus

In reflections twelve moons within your hands
The sky; the stars past within your mind
Who could capture the thoughts you hide?
Who could hold the stars within your hands?
Twelve moons shine within your life;
Flicker and die like the sun with no daylight
Like the son who had burnt too close to the sun
Fall of wings; or the fall of the dream of nights!

III

In the star drifted night; twelve moons lost insight
From the wolf that carried you through the trees
To the edge of your mind; to your own desire
To touch the space which only love creates!
To stare upon the throne that has been empty so long
To see your face on the warm summer breeze
To stop and search for the things we believe
Is to watch the moon flicker, fold around your life

IV

Life is the moons; when life is your soul,
On the window pane cracks start to show
Blue is the sky; when the light you hold within
Dark are the stars which never reflect your mind
Reflects the passage of the rooms of different sins
Your soul is the whole in which you must evolve
Time is a space in which we all race to capture life's sweet delight
Twelve stars; twelve moods within the light
A start or the beginning of an old life

Chorus

In reflections twelve moons within your hands
The sky; the stars past within your mind,
Who could capture the thoughts you hide
Who could hold the stars within your hands?
Twelve moons shine within your life;
Flicker and die like the sun with no daylight
Like the son who had burnt too close to the sun
Fall of wings; or the fall of the dream of nights

V

The thoughts of friends vanished and gone
The time we spent laughing in the sun
Wine that was spilt every night
A split in the moon; that never changes light
A bottle on the ocean that reflects the moons sun beat
Spirit of love which no one could every hold
A ghost running through our lives
A joker of time and place